TRUTH IN FOCUS

"A Practical Defense of the Christian Faith for Teens"

by Ryan P. Snuffer

FOREWORD BY NORMAN L. GEISLER

Acknowledgments

This text is dedicated to my children, Hannah and Luke, who represent the next generation of believers that will be called upon to defend their faith in increasingly trying times. Also, I will forever be indebted to the faculty at Southern Evangelical Seminary for sharing with me their expertise in apologetics and for exemplifying how to balance a stand for truth with a love for God and humanity. I also want to thank the faculty and students at Northside Christian Academy who were an integral part of the process of the development of this text.

Table of Contents

UNIT FOUR: THE IDENTITY OF CHRIST

UNIT FIVE: PRE-EVANGELISM AND EVANGELISM

UNIT SIX: RELEVANT ISSUES

Tables

Foreword

Defending the Faith is not an option; it is a command (1 Peter 3:15). Nowhere is this more important than among our teens — the next generation in training. Recent studies indicate that churches and Christian schools are failing to adequately prepare their teens to accept a biblical worldview. The result is that the church is losing this generation of young people to secular humanism, pantheism, or a very watered down version of Christianity. It would be over-simplistic to place all the blame on one particular area. However, one thing that demands our attention is in the matter of curriculum. Many Christian schools do not have some apologetics as part of the scope and sequence for Bible. However, many of those schools that include apologetics in their four year high school plan attempt a study without regard to the concept of absolute truth.

In this post-modern society, it is essential that students be trained to grasp the concept of absolute truth and be able to apply it to their view of the Bible, the world, and choices they make. Otherwise, they may merely conclude that Christianity is merely true for them but not for everyone.

Truth in Focus fills a much needed void in the world of high school texts currently available on the market. Ryan's practical approach will make learning to defend the Christian Faith more enjoyable and will motivate students to pursue a deeper study of apologetics throughout their lifetimes. Furthermore, it strikes a balance between faith and reason few high school texts have accomplished. *Truth in Focus* will not only help students to have a better understanding of truth, but will also equip them to make better choices related to faith and practice.

I believe God will greatly use this book in the years to come. It is clear, concise, and relevant. Few areas of Christian school curriculum are more needed than this one and no available book (and there are few) does a better job.

Norman L. Geisler

TRUTH IN FOCUS

UNIT ONE

INTRODUCTION AND TRUTH

Unit One: Introduction and Truth

Lesson 1
Introduction

Focal Points:

- To define apologetics
- To read and meditate on Proverbs 1:1-22
- To memorize and explain 1 Peter 3:15

Christian apologetics is a rational defense of the biblical faith. It is important for believers in Christ to be able to understand what they believe. Children usually accept what they are taught without question. As children get older, they begin to question their beliefs that they once assumed to be true. Some adults are uncomfortable when their children begin to question ideas that they have been taught. Some teens and adults may experience guilt when doubts arise in their minds because they have been conditioned to just accept what they are told without question. Furthermore, out of respect for the Bible, people may feel guilty about questioning God's Word. However, there is no law in the Bible that prevents people from thinking. God invites his people to reason with him (Is. 1:18). To question the interpretation of a passage in the Bible is not the same as doubting God. It is merely trying to understand and come to a knowledge of the truth. The study of apologetics goes beyond trying to understand what to believe and provides reasons to believe. It grapples with the "why" behind the "what."

When one takes a broad look at the Church throughout history and throughout the world today, one is faced with many different viewpoints about many different doctrines. However, there are several unifying doctrines that have been held by the vast majority of believers. These are reflected by the ancient church creeds as well as various doctrinal statements of churches today.

It is not realistic, nor even important for all Christians to reach a consensus of interpretation about all of the teachings of the Bible. On the other hand, it is important to know what is essential for a person to believe in order to be considered a Christian. It is primarily these "essential" beliefs of the Church that will be defended in this text.

Apologetics

1 Peter 3:15 states, "But sanctify the Lord God in your hearts, and always *be* ready to *give* a defense to everyone who asks you a reason for the hope that is in you, with meekness and fear."

This book uses a twelve point system that follows the classical approach to apologetics. The classical approach has been the dominant approach to apologetics at various times throughout church history. Kenneth Boa describes the classical approach as "rational" and that it "offers what its advocates consider *proofs* of various types (though especially philosophical proofs) for crucial claims of the Christian faith."[1]

Readers should become very familiar with these twelve points. They follow a logical progression of leading people from non-theistic worldviews to a point of decision about Jesus Christ. Although the Bible is the primary source of doctrine for the Christian faith, a person who is familiar with each of these points will be able to answer objections of people who have intellectual reasons for not accepting Jesus Christ as the Son of God, without using a Bible. This is an advantage when speaking with someone who does not respect the Bible as an inspired book. Ideally, we want to get people to the point that they desire to read the Bible for themselves. This is more likely to happen if people realize that the Bible is historically accurate and has relevance for them today. In this sense, apologetics is like pre-evangelism.

Some well-meaning Christians may ask, "Why not just use the Bible?" The answer is simple. There are some people who will not listen to the Bible. They shun the idea of being preached to or lectured. What power is in the claim to an atheist—that God loved the world so much that he gave His only Son? Furthermore, there are other people that are open to listening to or reading what the Bible has to say, but they do not believe that it is an inspired book any more than a story of Shakespeare or Steven King is a message from God.

The Holy Spirit is working in people's hearts and lives throughout the world. He often speaks through nature or a person's conscience. He speaks directly through the Bible. He speaks indirectly through believers. A good knowledge of apologetics will make a person a more useful ambassador for Christ.

No two people are exactly alike. For this reason, cookie cutter evangelistic approaches do not always work. They are often oversimplistic and take a one-size-fits-all approach to getting people to have a relationship with God. Furthermore, they can be insulting to people, especially in today's culture. People today don't want to be told what to do; nor do they want to be told how to believe. The classical approach is not as much about telling them what to think as it is helping them to think and facing them with logical truths. It is helping them to see that Christianity is worth believing because it is true. The most important reason to be a Christian is not simply to feel better or to gain friends or to be a part of something significant. The most important reason to be a Christian is because Christianity is true. Apologetics goes beyond simply telling a person that Christianity is true. It demonstrates with logic, reason, and the Bible that it is true, and therefore, worth believing.

Finally, this approach is more of an art than a science. In other words, it is not intended to be memorized and used to convert everyone in the same way. However, it is intended to equip the reader in such a way that when people ask questions, one can naturally transition into a conversation about God. It is also meant to become a part of the reader in such a way that when his faith is under attack, it does not crumble.

Conclusion

There was a time when most people in America believed in God and that the Bible was His Word. Today things are much different. Though most Americans still believe in God, their idea of God has changed dramatically. There are also more people who question God's authority or even his very existence. Agnosticism is an intellectual fad in some circles. With the internet and other forms of media, religious ideas of all sorts are readily available to all who inquire. Eastern religions and Islam are growing rapidly in the United States. If Christianity is going to prosper and grow, Christians need to be more certain about what they believe and why these beliefs are worth maintaining and defending.

Discussion Ideas

1. Do a study of 1 Peter 3:15 in its biblical context. Explain the significance of the phrases "be ready to give an answer to every man" and "with meekness and fear" from 1 Peter 3:15. Try using commentaries/Bible dictionaries/concordances in a group setting.

2. Read and summarize Proverbs 1:1-22. Record your thoughts in a journal. Distinguish between the wise person or the person who desires wisdom, and fools who despise wisdom.

3. Reflect on the changes in our society over the past fifty or sixty years and how these changes have impacted the need for a change in the way Christians try to fulfill the Great Commission.

4. List a few tough questions or difficult issues that you or someone you know have had about God or Christianity. Discuss ways in which these answers can be found.

Lesson 2
Why Study Apologetics?
(Part 1)

Focal Points:

- To list and explain reasons for studying apologetics
- To meditate on Proverbs 2:1-22 and to consider the value of wisdom
- To list biblical references that support the study of apologetics

The Bible commands it.

Though Christians may differ as to how to approach the subject of apologetics, they should not differ on the issue of whether they should study it or not. 1 Peter 3:15 clearly commands, "But sanctify the Lord God in your hearts: and *be* ready always to *give* an answer to every man that asketh you a reason of the hope that is in you with meekness and fear." The *New King James Version* renders the second phrase as "and always *be* ready to *give* a defense." It is this word "answer" in the *King James Version* and "defense" in the *New King James Version* that is translated from the Greek word "apologia," from which we get the word "apologetics." An accurate paraphrase of this verse is as follows: "Set God apart in your hearts and always be ready to defend your faith to any person who asks you why you believe, doing so in a spirit of humility and respect."

There are many other places in the Bible in which apologetics is either used or commanded. A study of apologetics will give believers the answers they need for many questions such as these. This book will introduce many topics that may inspire you to do further study.

Reason demands it.

People have many honest questions about faith and spirituality. Honest questions deserve honest answers. God created us in His image. Part of this image is our ability to think and reason. Questions that people have about Christianity include:

- How do we know that the Bible is true?
- Doesn't the Bible have a lot of mistakes after all the years of copies?
- How do we know that Jesus is God?
- Don't all religions lead to God in their own way?
- What makes Christianity better than any other religion?
- Is the Bible relevant to people today?
- Doesn't the Bible say that Christians shouldn't judge other people's beliefs?
- Is it possible to know anything with absolute certainty?

These are confusing times to be a Christian. With the plethora of interpretations among Christians about virtually every doctrine in the Bible, it is no wonder that so many young or new believers do not know what to believe, much less have reasons for their faith.

God created humans with the ability to reason. Because of man's depraved (sinful) nature, his ability to reason is often influenced by his rebellion against God. Yet, if a person is seeking the truth, and is willing to be intellectually honest, he or she can come to understand sound reason concerning spiritual things. Though people are totally depraved in a spiritual sense, they did not lose their ability to think reasonably when Adam sinned. A non-Christian can understand logic and reason as well as a believer.

In many cases, Christians are the ones that are not willing to think much about their faith. In fact, the perception of many outside of the church is that one must stop using his brain when walking into a church in order to experience God. The sad truth is that Christians have often given the un-churched reasons to believe this notion.

It is reasonable to want to know if there is evidence for the truth of Christianity since there are several prominent world religions with exclusive truth claims. A study of Christian apologetics will give reasonable answers and proofs for the central truth claims of Christianity.

Discussion/Assignments

1. Look up the following references. Point out a word or phrase in each verse or passage that demonstrates the use of apologetics.

   a. Matthew 22:29
   b. Acts 17:16, 17
   c. 2 Corinthians 10:5
   d. Philippians 1:7
   e. Titus 1:9
   f. Titus 1:13
   g. 1 John 4:1
   h. Jude 3

2. Notice the phrase from 1 Peter 3:15 that states, "to anyone who asks you." How often do people try to force their opinions on other people? This is true about many things in life, like who are the superior sports teams or best music bands. This is also true about religion. How do you think this phrase is consistent or inconsistent with the Great Commission found in Matthew 28:19, 20?

3. Think of a time in your life when you asked the question "why?" and you did not get a satisfactory response. Though there are times when it is not appropriate to ask this question, there are many times when it is appropriate to ask. Remem-

ber the frustration you felt when you asked this question and no answer was given. Try to imagine the frustration of non-Christians when they ask questions about God and get no solid answers. Perhaps you have been asked a question before about the Bible and you did not have a good answer to give. Write out several "why?" or "how do we know?" questions you have wondered about Christianity or the Bible before. Make it your goal to get the answers to these questions before you get to the end of your text.

Think: It would be interesting to record these questions and refer to them after you have completed this text. Ideally, many of your questions will be answered to your satisfaction. For those not answered adequately, there are recommended books listed throughout the text in which you can "dig a little deeper."

Lesson 3
Why Study Apologetics?
(Part 2)

Focal Points:

- To list and explain the three reasons for studying apologetics
- To read and list implications of current views on truth
- To define and give examples of moral relativism and moral absolutism

The world needs it.

The third reason that apologetics needs to be studied is because the world desperately needs it. The philosophical thinking of Americans has shifted in the direction of cultural and moral relativism over the past couple of generations. Francis Schaeffer asserts that the Christian must be acquainted with these shifts "if he is not equipping himself to work in a time period which no longer exists."[2] If Christians do not respond to these changes, then it will be difficult to make a lasting impact on their culture.

Schaeffer describes how the shift took place. In the United States, this shift was taking place around 1935. Before this time, everyone assumed that it was possible to know truth and that the opposite of true was false. The concepts of truth and non-truth were assumed. Philosophers struggled with finding a unity in the diversity—an ultimate truth that tied all the pieces of the universe together. One philosopher would draw a circle of truth and tell others they could live in it. Later, another philosopher would come along and cross the previous one out and draw a new one. New ones kept coming because of the lack of an absolute basis for any of them. Eventually people grew weary of systems of truth which did not connect with the real world. Schaeffer writes: "In the end the philosophers came to the realization that they could not find this unified rationalistic circle and so, departing from the classical methodology of *antithesis*, they shifted the concept of truth, and modern man was born."[3] What this means is that instead of dealing with a system of truth that distinguished between opposites such as right and wrong, a new system of truth was formed in which truth became whatever a person wanted it to be.

If Christians do not understand this shift, then our efforts to evangelize the world are futile. The world system is always changing. Each generation of Christians must learn to recognize this system, especially whenever it is in opposition to the Christian worldview. Each local church should put forth an effort to reach the people around it. To effectively reach these people requires faith, love, and an understanding of what they are thinking.

One of the greatest intellectual obstacles for Christians to overcome in western culture today is the denial of truth. Josh McDowell has compiled statistics of young people who attend church in America. He has found that many of them have distorted views about God and the Bible.[4]

> 65% want a close relationship with God
> 80% say their religious views are an important part of their lives
> 80% believe that God created the universe
> 87% believe Jesus was a real person
> 78% believe he was born of a virgin[5]

The above statistics show that there is hope. Yet, the following statistics should bring alarm to all who understand their implications.

63% believe that "Muslims, Buddhists, Christians, Jews, and
all other people pray to the same god."[6]

53% believe that Jesus committed sins

83% of teens maintain that moral truth depends on the circumstances, and only 6% believe that moral truth is absolute (2001).

Another poll indicates that when it comes to believing in absolute truth, only 9% of born again teens believe in moral absolutes
and just 4% of the non-born again teens believe that there are moral
absolutes.[7]

The generation raising these teenagers denies absolute truth to
a lesser degree. According to a Barna study, "By a 3-to-1 margin
(64% vs. 22%) adults said truth is always relative to the person and
their situation. The perspective was even more lopsided among teenagers, 83% of whom said moral truth depends on the circumstances,
and only 6% of whom said moral truth is absolute."[8]

When the various generations of adults are considered, the fact
that relativism is on the rise is evident. The same study concluded,
"While six out of ten people 36 and older embraced moral relativism, 75% of the adults 18 to 35 did so. Thus, it appears that relativism is gaining ground, largely because relativism appears to have
taken root with the generation that preceded today's teens."[9]

Though the numbers are better among professing born-again
Christians, there is still reason for concern.

Among adults, 32% of those who were born again said they
believe in moral absolutes, compared to just half as many
(15%) among the non-born again contingent. Among teenagers, there was still a 2-to-1 ratio evident, but the numbers
were much less impressive: only 9% of born again teens believe in moral absolutes versus 4% of the non-born again
teens.[10]

Unless Christians have a conviction that certain actions are right
or wrong, they have no basis to live a godly lifestyle. Biblical commands become optional suggestions. Belief in the Bible impacts

both doctrinal beliefs and moral decisions. Barna concluded that "substantial numbers of Christians believe that activities such as abortion, gay sex, sexual fantasies, cohabitation, drunkenness and viewing pornography are morally acceptable."[11] Barna statistics also reveal that the percentage of teens who hold to historic biblical Christianity has declined from 10% in 1995 to just 4% today.[12]

One important point to take from all these numbers is **the majority of people in our culture will need to be faced with their view on truth before you can effectively communicate with them about anything! Needless to say, it is difficult to convince a man that something is true if he does not know** what truth is.

God must be extremely grieved that so many who call themselves Christians have the beliefs and practices that they do. Likewise, it should grieve Christians that so many Christians fight with each other over trivial matters while allowing the world to stand by and watch in amusement or disbelief. Those who deny the person and work of Jesus Christ need to hear solid reasons to believe from those of us who do.

This generation has a tremendous task. Christians must decide what it is that is worth believing and then understand how to communicate these beliefs in such a way that unbelievers are willing to listen. The task may seem overwhelming. In fact, it is; however, you can claim the promise of Christ in Matthew 28:20—that He will be with you always. You have in your possession the power of God unto salvation for everyone who embraces it. Do not be ashamed. You have the truth that the world needs.

Discussion/Assignments

1. Imagine if you had been born in Saudi Arabia. Chances are you would be a Muslim today. What if you had been born into Hindu or Buddhist family? What if your parents and most of your friends were Jewish? It is not wise to accept any religion, even Christianity, just because it is the way you were raised. You need to consider the evidences for your own faith.

2. The statistics on the beliefs of Christian teenagers indicate that perhaps the average "Christian" teen is just as confused in his or her view of the world as the average non-Christian teen. Why do you think this is the case?

3. Define moral relativism and give examples of it in American culture.

4. Define moral absolutism and give an example of it in the church.

Recommended Reading

Josh McDowell, *Beyond Belief to Convictions*

Lesson 4
Three Reasons
People Reject Christ

Focal Points:

- To list the three reasons people reject God or Christ
- To answer the objections people have for rejecting God or Christ

There are many excuses people make for rejecting Jesus Christ as their Lord and Savior. These excuses can be summarized into three basic categories: volitional, emotional, and intellectual. Each of these categories requires a different approach when trying to share your faith.

Volitional

The first reason, volitional, is the most basic of all reasons and relates to the human will. People simply do not want to acknowledge who God is or submit to Him. Humans are sinners by nature. Romans 3:10 states, "There are none righteous, no not one." This theme continues through this chapter until verse 23 which states, "For all have sinned and come short of the glory of God." Since all humans are sinful and do not seek after God on their own, it could be said that all who reject God do so on some level for volitional reasons. All humans have a tendency to reject authority. It is more comfortable for some people to view God as an impersonal force or a distant idea. But if a person acknowledges that Jesus is the Son of God, he is forced to come to terms with his moral status and consider that certain changes need to take place. It is true that God has certain expectations of His people. It is this notion that keeps some people from accepting God.

There is nothing that we can humanly do to make a person believe in and accept God. However, we can maintain a faithful witness and look to the power of prayer and the Holy Spirit to bring about faith. Never underestimate the power of prayer. Pray that God would make His love known in the hearts of those who willfully reject Him.

Emotional

The second reason that many people reject Christ is emotional. People who reject God for emotional reasons are often difficult to connect with because we try to reach them with Bible verses or persuasive arguments alone. What they need is love and support to go along with the truth (Eph. 4:15).

For example, a lady may say that she rejects God because of all the suffering in the world. Perhaps she has lost a close loved one in a tragic painful event or to a dreadful disease. She feels that if God were real, that He would not allow these things to happen. Another example could be made of a guy who had an abusive father. He cannot imagine worshipping a Heavenly Father because of his warped view of fatherhood.

People who reject God because of the suffering of this world have a sense of justice. They recognize evil and do not like it. They might be comforted to know that God agrees with them and that one day God will put an end to it all (See lesson 21). Perhaps most importantly, People who have been hurt need our love and encouragement. They may also need instruction about God's attributes of love and mercy.

Intellectual

This third reason is the primary reason for this text. There are people who have legitimate questions about the truth of Christianity. These people deserve answers. In fact, the Bible commands us to give them answers. Many people have lived most of their lives in a non-Christian culture. What little they know of God or the Bible is inaccurate. They need apologetic type responses given in a tactful and loving manner.

Discussion/Assignments

Look at the following excuses from different people. Each of these people is rejecting belief in God or Christ as God. Explain what you believe would be the most appropriate way to share your faith with this person.

Table 1. Response to Excuses

Excuse:	Response:
1. God is too far away or too big to care about me.	
2. My mother suffered with cancer for many years before she died. She was a good person and too young to die.	
3. All religions have similar teachings and can lead to God.	
4. I want to go ahead and have fun for a few years before becoming a Christian.	
5. There are so many religions. How can we know if any of them are true?	
6. If God truly loved us, He would get rid of all the suffering in the world.	
7. I used to go to church. Most of the people there were hypocrites. Even the pastor got in trouble for immorality. I live a better life than most Christians.	

Focal point: Some of the above examples may be difficult to answer at this time. That is good for the reason that many people do not get interested in apologetics until they are challenged by an opposing view that they do not have an answer for. It is normal to struggle with these kinds of situations. Yet, these scenarios represent issues you will be faced with in real life some day. In real life, you will want to have solid answers.

Lesson 5
The Twelve Points

Focal Points:

- To memorize the six summary points of this apologetics model
- To relate the twelve points to various religious beliefs

In this study, we will look at a series of twelve points that can used to prove that Christianity is true. These were developed by Norman Geisler. They follow a logical progression from point to point. Each point is based on an understanding and an acceptance of the previous point. The twelve points are:

1. Truth about reality is knowable.
2. The opposite of true is false.
3. It is true that the theistic God exists.
4. If God exists then miracles are possible.
5. Miracles can be used to confirm a message from God.
6. The New Testament is historically reliable.
7. The New Testament says Jesus claimed to be God.
8. Jesus' claim to be God was miraculously confirmed.
9. Therefore, Jesus is God.
10. Whatever Jesus (who is God) teaches is true.
11. Jesus taught that the Bible is the Word of God.
12. Therefore, it is true that the Bible is the Word of God (and anything opposed to it is false).

It may seem tiresome to go through these points at first, but once you do, it will empower you to be able to be so much more effective in your life and ministry. It will equip you to be more effective in sharing Christ with others. It will strengthen your faith. You will be able to better withstand the attacks waged on Christianity by the media, by unbelieving family members and friends, and by secular minded professors in the college classroom.

These points will be developed throughout this book. Their logical progression will make more sense in time. Begin your mastery of them by memorizing the following six summary points:

1. Truth is absolute.
2. God exists.
3. Miracles confirm God's existence.
4. The Bible is reliable.
5. Christ is God.
6. The Word of God is true.

Discussion/Assignments

1. Go through each of the twelve points and notice how there is a logical progression in the order in which they are listed. The general idea is to take a person from a rejection of the Christian God to being ready to embrace the gospel message.

   a. At which of the twelve points would you likely begin if you were talking to an atheist (claims to not believe in God)?
   b. To a Muslim (rejects the authority of the New Testament and the deity of Christ)?
   c. To an Orthodox Jew (rejects the authority of the New Testament)?
   d. To an unbelieving church member (one who uses the Christian name, but denies the essential teachings of Christianity)?
   e. To a Hindu or New Age adherent (believes that the universe is God)?

2. Begin memorizing this list. It may seem like a tedious task now, but it will make this subject much easier in the long run.

Lesson 6
Truth is Absolute

Focal Points:

- To define truth
- To prove that truth is absolute by applying the definition of truth to hypothetical situations or events
- To memorize John 14:6 and 17:17

1. Truth about reality is knowable.

It is possible to know truth. Though this statement may not seem very profound, the fact is, most people in Western culture do not live by this statement. Today's culture embraces various forms of relativism. (Relativism is the view in regards to truth that truth is not absolute—that it may change in reference to time, culture, or perspective). This is easily seen in the area of ethics and morality. Clichés such as "truth is relative" or "what is wrong for you isn't necessarily wrong for me" reflect where Americans are in their thinking.

Truth is that which corresponds to reality. The nature of truth as absolute is undeniable. What is real is what is true. Facts are true regardless of a person's opinion about the circumstances or their relation to the circumstances. The statement "two plus two equals four" is true regardless of whether a person agrees with it or not. There are an infinite number of possible answers to this math equation, but there is only one correct answer. Truth is narrow. There are many possibilities about where you *could* be as you read this paragraph, but there is only one place where you *actually* are at any given time.

Even though people try to live by a relativistic philosophy of truth, it is impossible to live by it consistently. A person may hear a woman say "I am cold" or "It is cold in here" and respond by saying "true for you but not for me." Yet this does nothing to prove relativism. The original statement is either true or false. The woman who is cold is speaking about her own situation. She is the reference point, not the listener. The person listening may actually be warm, but the statement was not in reference to the listener. It is absolutely true for the one speaking that she is cold (if she is being honest). By the way, if she is being dishonest, then her truth claim is absolutely false.

As a good sports commentator witnesses a winning shot by a particular player, he will state those facts as they unfold. The events of that game are absolute truth. Though other games may be going on at the same time, the commentator was a witness to the facts of that particular game with certain players at a specific time in history. In any other game the facts will be different. Truth is what is.

Discussion/Assignments

1. Think about how the following statements are absolute truth claims, even though someone might misunderstand them as relative truth claims. Keep in mind that there can be a difference in a truth *claim* and something that is *proven* to be true. A claim does not have to be true. A lie is absolutely false. If something is true, then it is absolutely true. For example, if letter "a" is true, then it is true for all people, not just the person saying it.

   a. The Bible is God's Word.

   b. That was a great movie we watched the other night!

   c. That restaurant has the best steaks in town.

   d. The English language is confusing for some people to learn.

Focal point: Notice that "b" and "c" above are opinion statements. These kinds of statements are often used as examples by people who try to insist that truth is relative. However, these kinds of opinion statements are not meant to be all-encompassing. For example, the person who made the statement beside "b" does not really believe that everyone in the world in every culture would agree with his statement. He is simply stating his opinion about the movie. If he is being honest, then his statement is absolutely true concerning his opinion of the movie.

2. Truth is absolute; however, our perception of truth is not. People see things from different perspectives. One person may see the color blue slightly different than other people. But the properties that make something blue are what they are, regardless of how different people perceive them. How does this form of relativism differ from a relativism that looks at truth as relative (blue isn't really blue)?

3. Find a newspaper/magazine article that deals with a current ethical issue (such as gay marriages, abortion, euthanasia, etc.). Find one from a non-Christian perspective and try to notice if you can pick up on relativistic truth claims. These will sometimes be subtle and will require a discerning mind to notice.

   Be careful not to assume you know what the writer means unless you are sure. Sometimes statements will be blatantly obvious and will not be difficult to find at all. Once you have found such an article, critique it based on things you know about truth. If you are using this book in class, perhaps your teacher would give you extra credit to compose a letter to the writer of the article and send it to him or her. You should not critique the person for having a different perspective than yours. If you think that there is an unfair or dishonest bias, point it out. Name calling or demeaning words are unprofessional and will not be taken seriously. Understand the importance of using factual information rather than opinions in critiques. Here is a sample format you may choose to use:

1. Name of article, author, and source.
2. One sentence summary
3. What is it in the article that motivated you to write this letter?
4. In the letter, try to find something positive to say about the article; kindly refute any misrepresentation of the facts, unfair bias, or illogical arguments.

Recommended Reading

Norman L. Geisler, *Christian Apologetics*
Norman L. Geisler and Frank Turek, *I Do Not Have Enough Faith to be an Atheist*

Lesson 7
The Law of Non-Contradiction
and Three Worldviews

Focal Points:

- To define the law of non-contradiction
- To list and define the various worldviews

2. The opposite of true is false.

If truth is that which corresponds to reality then it follows that what is not reality is not true. The opposite of what is true is false. This may seem like a "no-brainer" and it should. This is sometimes referred to as the law of non-contradiction. This is a principle of logic which is one of twelve undeniable foundations of knowledge.[13] The law of non-contradiction states that direct opposites cannot both be true at the same time and in the same sense. The only way to deny the law of non-contradiction is to argue that opposites can both be true at the same time or in the same sense. Yet, this claim is self-defeating because it assumes that the opposite of the claim is false.

To apply the law of non-contradiction to the study of apologetics requires a look at the claim that God exists. Either God exists or He does not. Both claims cannot be true. If two worldviews make opposite claims about God's existence, they cannot both be correct about that claim. The thousands of religious and philosophical groups worldwide can be categorized into three basic worldviews.

Notice in Table 2 how these very basic worldviews contradict each other on the question of God.

Table 2. Three Worldviews

Worldview	Theism	Atheism	Pantheism
Question of God	God created all (personal)	No God at all	God is all (non-personal)
Examples	Christianity, Islam, Judaism	Atheism, Agnosticism, Secular Humanism	Hinduism, Buddhism, New Age

Only one of these worldviews can be true about the existence of God since they contradict each other on this point. If theism is correct about God, then atheism and pantheism are incorrect about God. It is important at this point to not jump to conclusions beyond what the logic provides. For instance, if it is true that a personal God exists, it does not automatically make everything that theists believe right about everything. Also, even if atheism and pantheism are wrong about the nature or existence of God, this does not mean that everything about atheism or pantheism is wrong. For instance, there may be elements of Hinduism that have something to contribute to our own religious pursuits; however, the Hindu view of God is impersonal. The theistic view of God is personal. These are opposites. Both views cannot be right on this point.

Some try to prove Christianity to be true by attempting to disprove the validity of all of the other major religions and worldviews. Although this approach may have merit, it is not the approach taken in this book. It is not necessary; any point or truth claim that is proven to be true will automatically disprove other truth claims that are in direct contradiction to it. Facts are facts. It can be proven that hybrid cars need less gasoline to run than older, conventional SUV's. To claim otherwise would be a false claim. Once a fact is established, anything in direct contradiction with the fact is false.

Discussion/Assignments

1. Practice applying various truth claims to themselves. For example, the comment "All truth is relative" is self-defeating. The answer could be "Is that a relative truth?" Obviously the person making the statement does not believe so. Try this technique with the following statements. Then try to think of other statements people in the world use and try to refute them using this technique.

   - There are no absolutes.
   - There is no truth.
   - That's just your interpretation.
   - You should not judge.
   - You should tolerate my belief—that all religions are equal.
   - No person or religion has the truth.

2. Write out the opposite of each of the following statements. Notice how the typed statement and its opposite cannot both be true in the same time and in the same sense.

   a. The Bible is the Word of God.
   b. Jesus is the only way to Heaven.
   c. The light is on.
   d. Pastor Smith spoke in chapel yesterday.

Focal point: The study of the Bible can be transformed from a boring task to one you can look forward to once you are able to see the connection between the information you must learn with the world in which you live. One "real world" idea that is predominant in this society is that it is possible that all three worldviews are true.

Recommended Reading

Paul Copan, *True for You, But Not for Me*
Ron Rhodes, *Challenge of Cults and New Religions*

Lesson 8
Faith vs. Reason?

Focal Points:

- To distinguish between faith and reason and the role of each in Christianity
- To recognize and create logical syllogisms
- To meditate on Isaiah 1:16-20

When a person becomes a Christian there must be faith present as well as an understanding of what it is that is believed. Faith is never without at least some knowledge. Even a child who comes to faith in Christ must have a certain amount of understanding of the facts of the gospel message in order to believe and accept these facts. It is faith in God that saves, not faith in faith. It is not enough to simply have faith. One must have faith in the truth of the gospel message and make a decision to receive these truths personally.

Faith

Hebrews 11:6 states that it is impossible to please God without faith. In Ephesians 2:8, 9 it states that a person is saved by faith apart from works. There are many things that must be accepted by faith in the Bible. For example, Hebrews 11:3a states, "Through faith we understand that the worlds were framed by the word of God." There is no human or scientific explanation that can adequately explain how the words of God could produce the universe that exists today. Yet the Bible says that it is true. The belief that God spoke the universe into existence is not blind faith. It is based on the testimony of the Bible. The Bible can be trusted because of reasons that are given later in this book.

Of course there is a limit to what humans can understand about the infinite nature of God as well as some of the ways of God. Again, this is where faith comes in. However, it is still not a blind leap of faith into the dark, but as we learn more about the accuracy and reliability of the Bible, we take bold steps of faith into the light. The Christian faith is based on reasonable truths.

Reason

The nature of man is imperfect and depraved and is therefore subject to faulty reasoning. Yet this does not take away man's ability to reason altogether. The Lord said to an unrepentant and rebellious audience in Isaiah 1:18, "Come now, and let us reason together, saith the Lord: though your sins be as scarlet, they shall be as white as snow." Paul reasoned with unbelievers in Acts 17:2, "And Paul, as his manner was, went in unto them, and three Sabbath days reasoned with them out of the scriptures." 1 Peter 3:15 commands believers to be able to give an answer to every man about the reason of the hope that is in them. It is clear from the Bible that sometimes it is necessary to use reasonable arguments when trying to reach others with the gospel of Christ.

Logic

One way to reason with other people is to use logical statements. The ancient philosopher Aristotle used logical syllogisms to prove various ideas and truth claims to his audiences. In the next few chapters, logical syllogisms will be used to provide evidence about certain truth claims. The structure of a simple logical syllogism is as follows:

1. *Premise*: Every six-legged creature with three body segments is an insect.

2. *Premise*: The Japanese Beatle has six legs and three body segments.
3. *Conclusion*: Therefore, the Japanese Beatle is an insect.

This is also know as deductive reasoning—moving from generals to particulars; from broad, inclusive truths to more narrow truths. The two premises should be provable and logically related to each other in order for the conclusion to be valid. It is possible for a syllogism to have more than two premises, but it must contain at least two. Notice the next syllogism that has three premises and a conclusion.

1. The Bible is accurate in every detail.
2. The Bible says that God cannot lie.
3. The Bible says that Jesus is God.
4. Therefore, it is true that Jesus cannot lie.

Faith and reason are both essential aspects of becoming a Christian and sharing one's faith effectively. Logical syllogisms are simply a way to help people communicate the truth logically. As you become more familiar with these concepts you will begin to think more logically, and become clearer in your communication of the truths of the Bible to those around you.

Discussion/Assignments

1. Practice correcting the following faulty syllogisms. Underline the incorrect part of the syllogism, explain why it is wrong, and make a correction to make it a true syllogism. The first one has been corrected for you as an example.

1. All dogs have four legs.
2. Cats have four legs.
3. Therefore, cats are really dogs.

The problem with the above syllogism is found in the conclusion. It is not a logical deduction from the first two premises. To make a correct syllogism, a third premise could be added that states that all animals with four legs are mammals. Then the conclusion could state that both dogs and cats are mammals.

1. All trees have leaves.
2. Dandelions have leaves.
3. Therefore, dandelions are trees.

1. Pencils have erasers.
2. That writing utensil has an eraser.
3. Therefore, all writing utensils are pencils.

1. God is holy and the source of all that is holy.
2. All religious people try to be holy.
3. Therefore, all religious people are godly.

2. Practice writing your own logical syllogisms.

TRUTH IN FOCUS

UNIT TWO

PROOFS FOR THE THEISTIC GOD

Lesson 9
Cosmological Argument

Focal Points:

- To define the cosmological argument
- To list examples of cause and effect and demonstrate the law of cause and effect in relation to the origin of the universe
- To refute the idea that God must have a cause for His existence
- To memorize Romans 1:19, 20

3. It is true that the theistic God exists.

Focal point: This lesson requires some deep thought. Some of the more philosophical or logical thinkers will appreciate this lesson more quickly than others. Make sure you understand this point clearly so that you can communicate it clearly to others. This writer has used the analogy of cause and effect with great success by drawing a series of arrows on the board pointing to other arrows. Each arrow represents a segment of time. The series must begin at a particular point. Even if you had an eternity to draw these arrows, you would never actually complete the task of drawing an infinite series. There had to be a first arrow drawn to begin the process.

There are several arguments that can be presented to try to prove that God exists and that theism is true. Three of the most important of these arguments will be studied in this text. It is important to be able to present arguments for God's existence without using the Bible. The atheist has every right to accuse a person of circular reasoning if he uses the Bible alone to prove that God exists. Some Christians believe that because the Bible is sufficient for all faith and practice, then one should never go outside of the Bible to prove spiritual matters. But the Bible itself teaches that there are sources of truth outside of itself that can teach people things related to God. Notice what the Psalmist writes:

> The heavens declare the glory of God; And the firmament shows His handiwork. Day unto day utters speech, and night unto night reveals knowledge. *There is* no speech nor language *where* their voice is not heard. Their line has gone out through all the earth, and their words to the end of the world. In them He has set a tabernacle for the sun, which *is* like a bridegroom coming out of his chamber, *and* rejoices like a strong man to run its race.[14]

Romans 1:19, 20 states,

> Because what may be known of God is manifest in them, for God has shown *it* to them. For since the creation of the world His invisible *attributes* are clearly seen, being understood by the things that are made, *even* His eternal power and Godhead, so that they are without excuse.

These passages teach that those who do not have Scripture can still know certain things about God—that He is eternal and powerful, and that the universe shows evidence of design (handiwork). One might say that God's existence is self-evident for those who want to know the truth.

In the next chapter of Romans the Bible teaches that a person's conscience has the law of God written on it.[15] In other words, every human has an innate sense of right and wrong. No appeal to Scripture is necessary to prove this fact. The first argument for the existence of God is the Cosmological Argument. This argument teaches that:

1. Everything that had a beginning had a cause
2. The universe had a beginning
3. Therefore, the universe had a cause.

The Cosmological argument answers the question of why there is a universe. It is there because God caused it to exist. Everything in nature is subject to the law of cause and effect because everything in nature had a beginning. God is not subject to the law of cause and effect because He had no beginning. He is an uncaused, necessary being. Though everything within the universe is bound to the laws of nature, since God is transcendent of nature, He is not bound to its laws. God is supernatural.

The naturalistic idea of the Big Bang as the cause of the universe is logically impossible without God. If there is no God, one must wonder "what caused the Big Bang?" Since everything that has a beginning has a cause, if the universe began with the Big Bang, it must also have had a cause. Yet if there is not a supernatural power beyond the physical universe, then the universe could have had no cause. Yet the universe does exist, therefore it must have had a cause.

The only way out of this logical dilemma is to postulate the idea of a universe that has always existed (infinite time), or an infinite number of universes that gave birth to each other (infinite series of causes). Stephen Hawking theorizes that the universe has been forever expanding and contracting. The universe is not singular, but a series of multiple histories.[16]

The idea of an infinite series of time or causes is logically impossible. An infinite regress in time is not possible because one would never arrive at the present. There must have been a First Cause to start everything. An infinite series is possible in the abstract, mathematical world. A potential infinite series is also possible in the future. But one will never arrive there, because there would always be more moments to traverse. According to Geisler, "Such a series, however, would not be actually infinite but only potentially infinite.

That is, it would never be complete, always being capable of having one more added to the series."[17] It is not possible for finite matter, limited to time, to traverse an actual infinite series in time. Therefore, it is not possible for matter to exist forever in past history.

Since the universe cannot be infinitely old, it must have had a beginning. If it had a beginning, it must have had a cause. This must have been the First Cause. Only a being that is uncaused and necessary can qualify as the First Cause. The only logical conclusion is that an eternal, transcendent, all-powerful God created the universe.

Discussion/Assignments

1. The atheist has no answer to the question of *why* something exists rather than nothing at all. Think about this statement and discuss its significance.

2. Look around the room. List five to ten items and what caused them to exist as they are. Then choose one of these items and trace back the causes all the way to God. This can be done with any item since God is the First Cause of the universe.

3. Read the first two chapters of Genesis. Count how many times the law of cause and effect is demonstrated and list a few examples.

4. The renowned atheist Bertrand Russell wrote concerning the Cosmological argument, "If everything must have a cause, then God must have a cause. If there can be anything without a cause, it may just as well be the world as God, so that there cannot be any validity in that argument."[18] Point out two things wrong with the reasoning of this statement. Then give an apologetic response.

Hint: By definition, God is supernatural. Only things of the natural world that have a beginning are subject to the law of cause and effect. Though angels and demons are not limited to the natural world that we can see, they are creatures with a beginning. Their existence is probably transcendent of the three dimensions that humans can comprehend, but they are not transcendent of the universe in the same way that God is.

Recommended Reading

Norman Geisler, *Baker Encyclopedia of Christian Apologetics*
Paul Little, *Know Why You Believe*

Lesson 10
Teleological Argument

Focal Points:

- To define the teleological argument
- To memorize Psalm 19:1, 2
- To meditate on Psalm 19:1-14

The teleological argument for the existence of God can be stated as follows:

1. Everything that has design must have a designer.
2. The universe shows evidence of design.
3. Therefore, the universe must have a Designer.

This argument is very simple. Every building has an architect; every watch has a watchmaker; every computer program has a programmer. If the universe indeed shows evidence for intelligent design, then there must be an intelligent Designer. There are many natural causes on earth such as winds, storms, erosion, and drought. Because there is intelligent life on earth, there are many intelligent causes as well. One can compare a sand dune to a sand castle to easily see the difference.

This argument is in direct opposition to Darwinian evolution. Secular humanism and Darwinism is propagated through every form of media possible. One means of spreading this philosophical dogma is through the college classroom, often in the name of science: "The history of life is not a story of immutable species individually created on a conservative planet, but is rather a chronicle of a restless Earth billions of years old, inhabited by a caste of living forms. Life evolves."[19]

This quote is from the first chapter of a popular college Biology book. It sets the tone for the entire semester. A Christian student who is taking this course will obviously have to separate his world views from the theme of this course. A couple of pages later another statement is even more aggressive: "Evolution is the core theme of Biology—a theme that will resurface in every unit of this text."[20]

Is evolution really the core theme of the study of life? One would think by these statements that all the issues concerning the origin of life have been settled and that no thinking person would challenge the theory of evolution. Some areas of study in science are revealing some serious problems with the theory of evolution. One of these is the idea of irreducible complexity.

Irreducible Complexity

Focal point: Look at a mousetrap. (Or other object that will serve this purpose). Notice how every part of this mousetrap must be designed to function properly if the unit is to function. Without a platform, there is no stability. With only a lever or a spring, the mouse would never get caught. All parts must work together simultaneously. None of the parts on their own could catch a mouse.

There are scientists, both Christian and non-Christian, who recognize some of the shortcomings of the evolutionary theory. Some have written books that challenge these views. One such man is professor of Biochemistry, Michael Behe, at Lehigh University. He has written a controversial book entitled *Darwin's Black Box*. The theme of this book is a concept he refers to as "irreducible complexity." He writes, "By *irreducibly complex* I mean a single system composed of several well-matched, interacting parts that contribute to the basic function, wherein the removal of any one of the parts causes the system to effectively cease functioning."[21] An illustration of this is of a mouse trap. The mouse trap includes several interactive parts which must be set by an outside force. The platform, the pin, the spring, and the lever are all important parts that must be placed together in a specific fashion if the trap is going to work successfully. If any one of these parts is removed, the trap will not do what it is designed to do successfully. In other words, each part on its own has no purpose in catching mice, but together they make a very effective means of catching an unsuspecting mouse.

Behe gives several examples of irreducible complexity throughout his book. One of the more familiar examples is of the human eye. He argues that the eye could not have evolved over a long period of time. Each of the parts is interdependent. These parts alone serve no purpose; together they give sight. He writes, "Since natural selection can only choose systems that are already working, then if a biological system cannot be produced gradually it would have to arise as an integrated unit, in one fell swoop, for natural selection to have anything to act on."[22] The possibility of this happening is infinitesimally small. This would require great leaps in evolution. Rather than small mutations, large rapid changes would need to have occurred. Yet, there is no evidence at all that anything can evolve in this way. Rather, the evidence is that the human eye was designed by an intelligent Designer.

Design in the Heavens

In our own solar system there is evidence for design. There are so many variables that must all fit into place to make human life possible. At 93,000,000 miles away, the distance of the earth from the sun is perfect for life. If it were much closer, it would be far too hot for human life. If it were any farther away, it would be much too cold. There is just enough oxygen and carbon dioxide in the atmosphere to form a perfect balance to sustain animal and plant life. Fresh water, minerals, and other natural resources are all essential to life. No other planet in the solar system resembles Earth with regards to its ability to sustain life. It may be true that no other planet in the universe has the perfect harmonious design that Earth has that makes such life possible.

Another evidence for design in the universe is the balance between opposing forces in the universe. For example, centrifugal force perfectly balances the gravitational force of traveling celestial bodies. One writer explains this phenomenon:

> The outward force of spinning solar systems and galaxies precisely balances the inward tug of gravitation. . . . As a result of this inexplicable balance, everything in the universe that revolves is kept from crashing in on itself, from this solar system to the farthest galaxy. And everything in the universe is revolving, as if in a never-ending waltz.[23]

Stephen Hawking comments on the attempt of science to find a unifying factor among all the complexities of the universe. He writes,

> Even if there is one possible unified theory, it is just a set of rules and equations. What is it that breathes fire into the equations and makes a universe for them to describe? The usual approach of science of constructing a mathematical model cannot answer the questions of why there should be a universe for the model to describe. Why does the universe go to all the bother of existing?[24]

This is an interesting quote from one of the most brilliant minds of the modern scientific world. Though Hawking is by no means a Bible-believing Christian, he is honest about the evidence he has witnessed in his scientific studies for the need for a designer.

Design implies purpose. Evolution attempts to answer the question of "how" the universe came to be. Even there it falls short at times and leads to more questions than answers. It cannot answer the "why" because in a universe without an intelligent designer there is no "why." Life would be without purpose in a world without God.

The teleological argument proves that God is immeasurably intelligent. From the DNA molecule within man to the galaxies of space, there is evidence for design throughout the universe. This argument also brings meaning to man's existence. His Creator designed him for a distinct purpose. He is considered important by his Creator. Just as every computer software program has a purpose originating in the mind of human programmers, every human being has a purpose originating in the mind of God. This thought makes life worth living and a study such as this worth pursuing.

Discussion/Assignments

1. There is an abundance of evidence of design throughout the universe. Since design implies God created with a purpose in mind, how can the Teleological argument help people realize their importance as human beings?

2. Take a walk outside (either literally or in your mind) and make a list of examples of design in the world around you. Make a distinction between things in nature designed by God and those in the world designed by man.

3. Read Paul's sermon in Acts 17. Describe his apologetic approach as he preached to these pagan listeners.

Recommended Reading

Michael Behe, *Darwin's Black Box*
Kenneth Boa and Robert M. Bowman, Jr. *Faith Has Its Reasons*

Lesson 11
Moral Argument

Focal Points:

- To define and explain the moral argument.
- To memorize Romans 2:14, 15

The moral argument is stated as follows:

1. For every law, there is a lawgiver.
2. There is a universal moral law in the world.
3. Therefore, there must be a universal Lawgiver.

The fact of the moral law is one of the major reasons C. S. Lewis converted to Christianity from atheism. He writes, "Human beings, all over the earth, have this curious idea that they ought to behave in a certain way, and cannot get rid of it."[25] It cannot be just some sort of herd instinct that has evolved over time for it is not always the desirable thing to do. In fact, it is usually easier to do the wrong thing. However, when a person does something wrong, he usually knows it. In any culture throughout the world it is wrong to murder or steal. Sometimes the specifics of what is wrong may be defined somewhat differently by different people. For example, some people define abortion as murder while others do not. Yet, they are not debating whether murder is right or wrong, only what murder is. Even people who are pro-choice generally do no see abortion as a good thing, but as the lesser of two evils or a choice that would be better avoided. The concept of murder or stealing something that rightfully belongs to someone else is taboo in any culture.

Many scientists are now suggesting that there is such thing as a "God gene." The theory is based on the fact that spirituality is "deeply woven into the human experience. . . . Spirituality is one of our basic human inheritances."[26] If there is a God gene, it was part of the Creator's design. The Bible speaks of knowledge of the law of God that was placed inside every human in Romans 2:14, 15.

Some societies have attempted to play God by setting their own boundaries of what is right and what is wrong. The Bible speaks of the possibility of having a seared or defiled conscience. For this reason, there may never be a unanimous agreement on every moral issue. However, the fact that everyone does live by a concept of right and wrong makes the moral argument very strong indeed.

A man who says he does not believe in a universal moral law will not live by this consistently. If he happens to be sitting on a park bench in the city and a thug walks up to him, assaults him, and steals his wallet, he knows instinctively that he has been wronged. He would have the same feeling if someone raped his wife or burned his house down. As soon as a person says "That isn't right" or "That is not fair" or "there is so much injustice in the world" he is proving that he believes in a standard of right and wrong. However, if he claims to not believe in God, the moral Lawgiver, there is no logical consistency for claiming to believe anything is intrinsically right or wrong.

The moral argument proves that there is a personal God and that He distinguishes between right and wrong. It implies that God is holy and is concerned that we live holy. It also can be a source of realization that we have upset God, by choosing to make choices that are in contradiction to this moral law. These three philosophical ideas can prepare the heart of a person to accept the next series of points in this manual, leading up to presenting the gospel of Christ.

These arguments should be learned so that you will be able to present them in your own words. You may do further studies and become very familiar with how to present these ideas in various situations. Do not be intimidated by those who do not agree with you on these points. You have the truth. Others are blinded by their unbelief, making it difficult for them to see the truth. Remember that it is ultimately God who must reveal Himself to them. You can present the truths. God must apply the truths in their hearts to produce faith.

Discussion/Assignments

1. Rewrite Romans 2:14, 15 in your own words in the space below.

2. Make a list of all the things a person can know about God based on the Cosmological, Teleological, and Moral arguments, without ever opening the Bible. Explain how these arguments could be a starting point for eventually leading someone to Christ.

3. Go back and look at the worldviews chart in lesson 3. Using the three arguments for the existence of God, and the law of non-contradiction, list four reasons that theism must be true and the alternatives must be false.

Recommended Reading

C. S. Lewis, *Mere Christianity*

TRUTH IN FOCUS

UNIT THREE

MIRACLES
AND THE NEW TESTAMENT

Unit 3:
Miracles and the New Testament

Lesson 12
Miracles

Focal Points:

- To demonstrate that if there is a God, that people should come to expect that miracles have indeed occurred
- To list examples of biblical miracles
- To meditate on Isaiah 61:1-3 and Luke 4:16-21

4. If God exists then miracles are possible.

The three philosophical arguments for God's existence demonstrate certain things about the person and nature of God related to His power and eternal nature (cosmological argument), His intelligence (teleological argument), and His moral nature (moral argument). If a God such as this truly exists, then it follows that this God can transcend His creation and act at will. The greatest act of God of all is the creation of the universe. Any other miracle is far less by comparison. If God created this universe then certainly it would be possible for him to transcend it—even to the point of revealing himself if He chose to. A miracle is an act of God, supernatural either in its essence or its timing.

Skeptics who deny the supernatural elements of the Bible are guilty of circular reasoning. They begin with an anti-supernatural bias. Then they systematically attempt to explain away the miracles of the Bible as myth. Their bias will always lead them to the same conclusion regardless of the evidence. They attempt to give naturalistic explanations for every alleged supernatural event, or they attempt to discredit those who claimed it happened.

One may suggest that the Christian is guilty of circular reasoning in the opposite way—that of a supernatural bias. But Christians do not need to begin with the presupposition that there is a God who can act without using any evidence to support this position. Even with just a brief look at the three arguments presented in this text one can see that there is evidence for a personal, powerful, eternal, intelligent, holy God who created us with a purpose. One does not have to go to the Bible to prove this. Some Christians may struggle with the idea that the Bible is not necessary to prove God's existence. Be assured that the Bible promotes this very idea. Psalm 19, Romans 1:19, 20, and Romans 2:14, 15 all give examples of how people can know certain truths about God without ever opening a Bible.

This is an important idea related to evangelism. If a person is coming from a perspective in which he has never given much thought to God or the supernatural, he is going to need some sort of evidence to convince him of God's existence and presence in the world. The Holy Spirit is ultimately the one that brings a person to faith; however, God uses people and the rest of creation to accomplish this process.

Once a person accepts the idea of the theistic God, it is easier for that person to believe that the Bible is the Word of God. Since the ultimate goal of apologetics is to defend the faith by giving people reasons to trust Christ as Savior, ultimately, reasons will be given to prove that the Bible is the Word of God. The next point on miracles is a crucial step in this process.

Discussion/Assignments

1. Skeptics try to offer naturalistic explanations for the miracles of the Bible. For example, they say that the feeding of the 5000 was an example of everyone pitching in and sharing their food with each other. Of course this contradicts the biblical description of this event; however, there are certain miracles of the Bible which could have no natural explanations. See how many you can think of and list them.

2. There are records in the Bible of counterfeit miracles (often occur in the name of magic or sorceries) that have occurred in the past as well as predictions of those that will occur in the future (2 Thess. 2:9; Rev. 9:21; 13:13). Who is behind these acts and what would be the purpose?

Lesson 13
Miracles
(Part 2)

Focal Points:

- To explain the connection between the miracle periods of the Bible and the revelation of God's Word
- To read and meditate on John 10:37, 38; 11:43-48

5. Miracles can be used to confirm a message from God.

If God chose to reveal Himself to mankind, it is likely that He would accompany the message with miraculous acts. The Bible records many miracles that were intended to validate the message of the prophets speaking or writing on behalf of God. There are three time periods recorded in the Bible that included many miracles. The table below illustrates how these time periods coincided with the writing of major portions of the Bible.

Table 3. Miracle Periods

Time Period	Moses-Joshua	Elijah-Elisha	Jesus-Apostles
Scripture Written	Genesis-Deuteronomy, Joshua.	Most of the Old Testament. These men initiated a time period that lasted for hundreds of years in which God used prophets to reveal His Word.	The entire New Testament
Miracles	Plagues in Egypt, parting of Red Sea, Ten Commandments	Causing the rain to cease, calling down fire from heaven	Healing sick, raising the dead, casting out demons

It is impossible to prove that there is no God, for one would have to be either omniscient (to know all things) or omnipresent (to be everywhere present) to prove this point. These are attributes unique to God. One would have to be God in order to prove that there is no God!

If there is a God, then miracles are not only possible, but probable. Since God created mankind with a distinct purpose, it is probable that God would reveal this purpose to him. The best way to do this would be in written form so that his message would be preserved for future generations. This is precisely what God did through the prophets and the apostles when He gave us the Old and New Testaments. The prophets and apostles needed some way to prove their credibility to a skeptical world that has so many other religious ideas to offer. God chose to use miracles as a means to authenticate their message. The miracles were varied in type and were usually performed in the presence of many eyewitnesses. People respected and listened to the prophets and apostles, in part, because of the miracles.

Miracles Today

There is a wide range of opinions within Christianity about the place of miracles in the church today. One thing is certain—God is able to perform miracles today, just like He did during other time periods. Their individual purposes may vary; however, the ultimate purpose would be what they have always been—for the glory of God. There is not new Scripture being recorded today. The Bible is complete. Therefore, there is no reason to believe that miracles would be used to authenticate new revelation of God. Nonetheless, God is still at work in His creation. He is actively involved in the lives of His people. God heals, comforts, teaches, and answers very specific prayers.

Conclusion:

God used miracles to authenticate His message as well as His messengers. The Bible was written during time periods in which many miracles were performed in the presence of many eyewitnesses. There is no reason to doubt the supernatural elements of the Bible if one believes in God. A God that can create a universe certainly has the ability and the right to intervene in that universe whenever and however He wills. The same God who performed miracles in the "Bible days" is still performing miracles today.

Discussion/Assignments

1. Though the majority of miracles of the Bible were limited to time periods in which portions of the Bible were being written, God can act whenever He desires in a miraculous way. Discuss examples of personal experiences in which it seems that God has intervened in lives today.

2. One might suggest that just as many miracles occurred at times other than the three big periods. The reason we know of these miracles is that they occurred during the times the Bible was being written. What do you think? Have you ever experienced anything in your life that had the feel of divine intervention?

3. Read and meditate on John 10:37, 38; 11:43-48; and 14:11. Notice that there were those who believed in Jesus because of the miraculous works He did. In fact, His miracles were an important part in establishing who He was. Why do you think that there were those who, despite having seen or heard of Jesus' miracles, continued to reject Him?

Lesson 14
The Bible is Reliable
(Part 1)

Focal Points:

- To list various proofs for the reliability of the transmission of the New Testament text
- To read and meditate on 1 Peter 1:17-25
- To memorize 2 Peter 1:20, 21

6. The New Testament is historically reliable.

There are very few religious books considered authoritative by its adherents which claim divine authorship. The major ones include the *Koran*, *The Book of Mormon*, and the Old and New Testaments of the Bible. Though the Bible is older than the other two, its reliability can be well-established.

These lessons will not attempt to prove the reliability of the Old Testament for three reasons. First of all, the accuracy of the Old Testament is not attacked as frequently as the New Testament. Secondly, the saving message of the gospel of Jesus Christ is more clearly presented in the New Testament. Thirdly, once the point is made that Jesus is the Son of God, it will be easy to prove the Old Testament's validity based on the words of Jesus. Jesus and the apostles affirmed the divine inspiration of the Old Testament.

The original manuscripts of the New Testaments are probably no longer in existence. However, this should not trouble Christians, for there are thousands of accurate manuscript copies. These manuscripts are hand-written copies of the New Testament that were written over a period of about 1400 years.

Accurate Copies

The amount of time between the original writings and the earliest known fragments is only about fifty years. Certainly some of the original or first generation copies would have still been in existence and accessible to anyone who wanted to compare them with each other. If the copies were not accurate, they could have easily been corrected when compared with the originals. When put side by side with other ancient documents, this gap is shown to be extremely small. Most other ancient documents have an average of about one thousand years separating them from their origins. Table 4 below illustrates this by comparing a few ancient documents.[27]

There are also more New Testament manuscripts than there are of any other ancient document. Well over 5700 manuscripts have been discovered to date. When these are compared to each other, there is an amazing consistency. Most of the inconsistencies can be attributed to scribal errors. When one examines all of the manuscripts, no doctrinal issues are threatened by the manuscript evidence.

Table 4. Ancient Manuscripts Comparisons

Author/Book	Date Written	Earliest Copies	Time Gap	No. of Copies
Demosthenes	300 B.C.	c. A.D. 1100	1,400 years	200
Caesar, *Gallic Wars*	100-44 B.C.	c. A.D. 900	1,000 years	10
Tacitus, *Annals*	A.D. 100	c. A.D. 1100	1,000 years	20
Plato	400 B.C.	c. A.D. 900	1,300 years	7
New Testament	A.D. 50-100	c. 114 (fragment) c. 200 (books)	50 years 100 years	Over 5,700

When one looks outside of the New Testament for support, there is found to exist over 18,000 non-Greek manuscripts and 36,000 quotations in ancient documents that support the accuracy of the New Testament manuscripts.[28] No other ancient document even comes close to having such an abundance of external evidential support.

It is puzzling that anyone would question its accuracy, since the New Testament has earlier, more numerous, more accurately copied and more abundantly supported manuscripts than any other ancient document in the history of the world. If the New Testament cannot be trusted, then no other ancient document in the history of the world can be trusted. Yet critics do not widely question the major works of the Greek philosophers or many other ancient writings.

Some of those who attack the Bible will point out that there are thousands of errors in the manuscripts. This is a misleading statement in light of the fact that these numbers are compiled by looking at the thousands of different manuscripts. If each manuscript had one error in it, that would easily account for over 5000 mistakes! If one early copy had a word or phrase missing, then all those manuscripts that are copied from this early manuscript might have the same mistake. This should be counted as one mistake, yet skeptics might refer to all of the manuscripts with this same error in it and say that this represents hundreds of mistakes. Some mistakes are mere spelling errors. Once can look at the abundance of manuscript evidence and recognize the original wording or phrase in question.

The most important thing to realize while discussing all these alleged mistakes is that none of them are in reference to the originals. It is the claim of this text, and all who profess biblical Christianity that the original manuscripts had no mistakes whatsoever. It is also important to point out that while most all of the errors in individual manuscripts are easily corrected, even if these verses or passages are considered questionable, one could still prove every point in this text as well as every essential doctrine of the Bible using passages that are not in question.

Though one may not want to accept the message of the Bible, it would not be intellectually honest to say that there is not abundant evidence for an accurate transmission of the text of the New Testament. Whether the originals can be trusted or not is a question the next lesson will attempt to answer.

Discussion/Assignments

1. Meditate on 1 Peter 1:23-25 and 2 Peter 1:17-21. Consider the following question and then record your thoughts in a journal. If God chose to reveal information about Himself and have it recorded in the Bible, why would He not also oversee the manuscripts throughout history to ensure that His message would not be corrupted or lost?

2. One student should copy a paragraph chosen from an unfamiliar source by the teacher. Three students should hand copy this paragraph on their own. Then have three or more students make copies from each of the three copies. After making several generations of copies, have students compare the newest copies with each other. It is probable that a few spelling errors will have crept into the newer copies. See if students can reconstruct the original paragraph into a word perfect, letter perfect format.

   This illustrates how copies of the Bible were transmitted through the generations before the printing press. It is important to understand that the scribes took their task very seriously and there were very few of these types of errors. By comparing the various manuscripts, it is not difficult to recognize the original reading.

Recommended Reading

Paul Little, *Know Why You Believe*
Josh McDowell, *Evidence that Demands a Verdict*
Norman Geisler and Frank Turek, *I Don't Have Enough Faith to be and Atheist*

Lesson 15
The Bible is Reliable
(Part 2)

Focal Points:

- To list proofs for the reliability of the original New Testament text
- To read and meditate on Luke 1:1-3.

Accurate Originals

It is important to demonstrate that the transmission of the text from the time of the originals to the present time has not allowed for a significant corruption of the text. But what good is a faithful preservation of the original if the original cannot be trusted? There happens to be good reasons to believe that the originals **can** be trusted. Here are just a few.

Eyewitnesses

The New Testament was written by eyewitnesses. An eyewitness account is the most important way to validate truth. Some may suggest that the gospels are biased because they were written by eyewitnesses, but eyewitnesses are the most qualified to give an accurate account of the historical details. In a court of law, an eyewitness account is considered solid evidence today.

There is evidence that the eyewitnesses did not collaborate with each other. For instance, they wrote about the same events, but recorded different details of those events. Though the different accounts complement each other to present a fuller picture of history, sometimes the accounts differ to the point that they seem at first to contradict one another. These discrepancies usually can be explained very easily. Norman Geisler and Thomas Howe have written a very helpful book that deals with most of the alleged discrepancies in the entire Bible and explains them.[29] Rather than casting doubt on the authenticity of the Bible, these apparent discrepancies indicate that the writers did not get together to make sure that their stories were consistent. If the disciples were conspiring to start a new religion, they would have been much more careful to make sure the stories did not contain these alleged discrepancies.

Furthermore, these eyewitnesses recorded personal weaknesses and mistakes. They were not trying to make themselves heroes. They simply recorded history, whether it made them look good or not. If they were trying to fabricate a story, they would have likely excluded details that revealed their own personal mistakes.

External Writings

It is also important to mention that non-Christian writers and archaeology confirm what the New Testament says. According to Geisler, there are several credible non-Christian sources including historians such as Josephus and Tacitus and government officials such as Pliny the Younger that affirm the historicity of Jesus and the record of the disciples (though they did not always agree with the beliefs of the disciples). For example, the Babylonian Talmud claims that Jesus worked magic and was hanged on Passover Eve. Pliny wrote that Jesus' followers worshipped Him as God.[30]

Bible scholars have studied writings other than the Bible that date back to the time of the first century that affirm the truths of the Bible. They have found that these sources together include the following facts:

- Jesus lived during time of Tiberius Caesar.
- He lived a virtuous life.

- He was a wonder-worker.
- He had a brother named James.
- He was acclaimed to be the Messiah.
- He was crucified under Pontius Pilate.
- An eclipse & earthquake occurred when He died.
- He was crucified on the eve of the Passover.
- His disciples believed He rose from the dead.
- His disciples were willing to die for their belief.
- Christianity spread rapidly as far as Rome.
- His disciples denied the Roman gods and worshiped Jesus as God.[31]

Archaeology Affirms the Bible

An entire course could be taken just on this one point. Archeological studies have demonstrated the historical accuracy of the Bible time and time again. Even secular writers agree with this point. One journalist noted, "In extraordinary ways, modern archaeology has affirmed the historical core of the Old and New Testaments—corroborating key portions of the stories of Israel's patriarchs, the Exodus, the Davidic monarchy, and the life and times of Jesus."[32]

It can also be said that no archeological discovery has ever contradicted a teaching of the New Testament. If the New Testament were not historically accurate, this would be one area that would result in problems, but it never does.

Writers Persecuted

The strongest evidence that the writers were writing factual history is that they were persecuted and killed for what they wrote and affirmed. Though men may die for a lie, they will rarely die for something they *know* to be a lie. When Muslim terrorists commit suicide in the name of Jihad, they believe that they will be rewarded in Paradise for their deed. They believe in a lie. Yet, they have no tangible proof that what they believe is true. However, the 1st century disciples of Jesus were eyewitnesses of the events they recorded in Scriptures. They were persecuted and died for their written and spoken testimonies.

One can safely conclude based on these points that have been touched on briefly that the New Testament is historically reliable. It is factual, not mythical. When it records an event, we can be assured that the event truly happened. When it records a conversation or a sermon from Jesus, one can safely assume that the writers were faithful in recording what was said.

Discussion/Assignments

1. Notice the first few verses of Luke chapter one and describe how Luke was able to gather his information.

2. Luke was the one gospel writer who was probably not an eyewitness to the events recorded in the gospel. Read through Luke 1-3 and record all the times Luke records people's names, places, dates, and events.

3. In the same three chapters of Luke, notice how Luke interweaves the events that are natural with those that are supernatural without any change in the way the events are described.

4. Show a five minute DVD recording and have people carefully record the details of the story. Collect the records. Type four of them onto a PowerPoint presentation or photocopy for comparison. Review the four accounts. Notice how they complement each other. Together, the four accounts should result in a more complete account than any one on its own.

   It is possible that human error would allow mistakes into the accounts, but The Holy Spirit ensured that no mistakes would enter into the final text of Scripture. This point will be developed in more detail later.

TRUTH IN FOCUS

UNIT FOUR

THE IDENTITY OF CHRIST

Unit 4: The Identity Of Christ

Lesson 16
The Deity of Christ

Focal Points:

- To list and/or memorize several references in the Bible in which Jesus made a claim to deity
- To explain C. S. Lewis' three options concerning the identity of Jesus Christ.
- To memorize John 20:28, 29

7. The New Testament says Jesus claimed to be God.

Since it has been demonstrated that the New Testament can be trusted, examining its contents is the next logical step. Since the person and identity of Jesus Christ is fundamental to Christianity, it is important to look at who He said He was. In the New Testament, Jesus made several distinct claims to deity. The following is a list of a few of the instances in which Jesus made a claim to deity. These verses are related to the title "I am" attributed to Jehovah in the Old Testament.

1. John 8:58 Jesus said to them, "Most assuredly, I say to you, before Abraham was, I AM."
2. John 8:24 "Therefore I said to you that you will die in your sins; for if you do not believe that I am *He,* you will die in your sins." See also John 13:19.
4. John 6:35 "I am the bread of life."
5. John 8:12 "I am the light of the world." (See Ps. 27:1)
6. John 10:9 "I am the door of the sheep."
7. John 10:11 "I am the good shepherd." (See Ps. 23:1)
8. John 11:25 "I am the resurrection and the life."
9. John 14:6 "I am the way, the truth, and the life."
10. John 15:1 "I am the true vine."

In Exodus 3:14, after Moses had asked God who he should say had instructed him concerning the deliverance of the people out of Egypt, the Lord said, "I AM WHO I AM." And He said, "Thus you shall say to the children of Israel, 'I AM has sent me to you.'" When Jesus used this title to identify himself, it was a clear claim to be Jehovah God of the Old Testament. Following this claim, the Jews took up stones to stone Him for blasphemy. This actually happened on several occasion after Jesus made claims about His identity. For example, John 10:30-38 states,

"I and *My* Father are one." Then the Jews took up stones again to stone Him. Jesus answered them, "Many good works I have shown you from My Father. For which of those works do you stone Me?" The Jews answered Him, saying, "For a good work we do not stone You, but for blasphemy, and because You, being a Man, make Yourself God." Jesus answered them, "Is it not written in your law, 'I said, "You are gods"'? If He called them gods, to whom the word of God came (and the Scripture cannot be broken), do you say of Him whom the Father sanctified and sent into the world, 'You are blaspheming,' because I said, 'I am the Son of God'? If I do not do the works of My Father, do not believe Me; but if I do, though you do not believe Me, believe the works, that you may know and believe that the Father *is* in Me, and I in Him."[33]

It was clear that the Jews interpreted this statement as Jesus claiming equality with God. Rather than correcting the Jews, Jesus affirmed their interpretation.

John 17:5 is a significant claim to deity for Jesus claimed to share with the eternal glory belonging to the Father. In this verse Jesus is quoted as saying, "And now, O Father, glorify Me together with Yourself, with the glory which I had with You before the world was." Jesus also accepted worship on many occasions (Matt. 8:2; 9:18; 14:33; 15:25; 20:20). Both testaments of the Bible are clear that only God should be worshipped (Exod. 20:1-4; Deut. 5:6-9; Rev. 22:8, 9).

According to Mark 14:61-64, the reason Jesus was put to death was because of His claim to be the Son of God. After His resurrection, Jesus was referred to as God by one of His disciples when Thomas said, "My Lord and my God!" Jesus said to him, "Thomas, because you have seen Me, you have believed. Blessed *are* those who have not seen and *yet* have believed."[34]

The apostle John gives another clear affirmation of the deity of Christ in John 1:1-14. Jesus is referred to as the Word who is God in this passage and is described as the One who created everything in the world.

At this point, it should be crystal clear that Jesus claimed to be God. Either He is God in human form or He is not. If Jesus is not God, then He either lied about His identity or He was insane. C. S. Lewis stated that there are only three choices.

I am trying here to prevent anyone saying the really foolish thing that people often say about Him: 'I am ready to accept Jesus as a great moral teacher, but I don't accept His claim to be God.' That is the one thing we must not say. A man who was merely a man and said the sort of things Jesus said would not be a great moral teacher. He would either be a lunatic—on a level with a man who says he is a poached egg—or else he would be the Devil of Hell. You must make your choice. Either this man was, and is, the Son of God: or else a madman or something worse. You can shut Him up for a fool, you can spit at Him and kill Him as a demon; or you can fall at His feet and call Him Lord and God. But let us not come with any patronizing nonsense about His being a great human teacher. He has not left that open to us. He did not intend to.[35]

Jesus is either who He said He was, or Christianity falls apart. If Jesus is not God then He is not worth listening to at all, for He is either a liar or a lunatic. Some have suggested a fourth option—that the entire story is just a legend. However, one finds this option to be impossible once the evidence is examined for the accuracy of the New Testament. Remember, there is more evidence for the historical Jesus and the accuracy of the New Testament than any person and writing from the ancient world. The following lesson will discuss evidences that Jesus was who He said He was.

Discussion/Application

1. The identity of Christ is central to Christianity. If Jesus is God, then everything He says is absolutely true. You could say that if Jesus is God, then Christianity is true. If Jesus is not God, then Christianity is false and should be rejected.

2. Each of the "I am" statements Jesus made have significance rooted and grounded in Old Testament teachings the Jews were familiar with. Do a research project using concordances and other study aides to help you find concepts in the Old Testament that relate to each of these statements. This could be done individually or as a group project with each group studying one or two of the sayings.

   For example, the good shepherd could be related to Psalm 23 and the cultural practice of that day. The bread of life could be related to the provision of manna for the Jews in the wilderness wanderings. The tabernacle furnishings are typified in Christ.

a. John 8:58 "Before Abraham was, I AM."
b. John 6:35 "I am the bread of life."
c. John 8:12 "I am the light of the world." (See Ps. 27:1)
d. John 10:9 "I am the door of the sheep."
e. John 10:11 "I am the good shepherd." (See Ps. 23:1)
f. John 11:25 "I am the resurrection and the life."
g. John 14:6 "I am the way, the truth, and the life."
h. John 15:1 "I am the true vine."

3. Explain C. S. Lewis's trilemma challenge.

4. What are the doctrines of Christianity that are necessary to the Christian faith? Make a list as you discuss these as a group. Look at your local church's doctrinal statement. Most churches will publish this on their website. Which of these doctrines can be considered essential?

Application: *Christians cannot compromise the essentials of the faith. Though the non-essentials may be important, we can learn to agree to disagree in a spirit of humility and love.*

Lesson 17
The Credentials that
Support Jesus' Claim

Focal Points:

- To defend Jesus' claim to deity
- To list Scripture references to support that Jesus was sinless
- To memorize John 1:1, 14 and meditate on John 1:1-18

It is now clear that Jesus claimed to be God. Though He is not the only person in history to make this claim, He is the only leader of a major world religion to make this claim. It is important to take a close look at His life to see if He lived the kind of life to back up this shocking claim.

8. Jesus' claim to be God was miraculously confirmed.

There are many ways in which Jesus' identity is tied to miraculous confirmation. These confirmations can be divided into the following three categories:

a. Fulfillment of prophecies about Himself;

b. Sinless and miraculous life;

c. Prediction and accomplishment of His resurrection

Any one of these three could easily be enough proof for Jesus' divinity. Together, they proclaim loud and clear that Jesus is who He said He was — the one and only God.

Fulfillment of prophecies about Himself

The Old Testament is full of prophecies concerning the future of Israel. Hundreds of these were specific references to the coming Messiah of Israel who would be their savior.

These prophecies demonstrate that the Messiah of Israel would be born of a virgin (Isa. 7:14), would be born in Bethlehem (Mic. 5:2), would perform miraculous signs in His life (Isa. 61:1), would be rejected by His own people (Isa. 53:3), and would be persecuted and killed (Isa. 53). Psalm 22 is interesting for the reason that seemingly insignificant details of His death are predicted about 1000 years in advance. This passage mentions that the Messiah would be mocked (Ps. 22:7, 8) and that His hands and feet would be pierced (Ps. 22:16). These were fulfilled at the time of the crucifixion of Christ.

Many more examples could be given. The last book of the Old Testament was written over four hundred years before the fulfillment of these prophecies. The discovery of the Dead Sea Scrolls confirmed that these were written as prophecies rather than as history after the fact. The probability that even a handful of these prophecies could be fulfilled by chance is so high that few who take an honest look at the evidence will be able to refute its claims.

His sinless and miraculous life

Jesus lived a morally perfect life. Peter testified in 1 Peter 2:22 that Jesus had "committed no sin, nor was any deceit found in His mouth." Not even his accusers could find any moral fault in Him. He was put to death because of His claim to deity, not because of any crime.

The gospels record many miracles of Jesus. Many of these are familiar to millions of people who attended Sunday school as a child. These are not just stories, but actual events that occurred in history. In fact, Jesus did many more amazing feats than just those that are recorded in Scripture. The gospel writer John closed his book with these words: "And there are also many other things that Jesus did, which if they were written one by one, I suppose that even the world itself could not contain the books that would be written."

Discussion/Assignments

1. Modern day prophets and psychics have given some people the impression that predicting the future is not an uncommon gift. However, none of these modern day seers measure up to the biblical standards of a prophet. Deuteronomy 18:15-22 states that the prophet must come in the name of God and that every prophecy must come to pass. No amount of guesswork or demonic power can come even close to 100% accuracy. A study of modern day psychics will reveal that most of them are more than 90% wrong! Many of their prophecies are so vague that there could be several possible interpretations. To demonstrate the difficulty in guessing the future, try to guess the exact final score of two or three games coming up over the weekend.

   My predictions: _____ _____ _____

   Actual scores: _____ _____ _____

2. The following chart demonstrates the progressive unfolding of the person of Christ from a prophetic viewpoint. The first prophecy of the Messiah was given in the Garden of Eden shortly after the first sin. Genesis 3:15 indicates that the Messiah would be born of a woman. Later in Scripture the prophets describe Jehovah as the only Savior (Isaiah 43:11). It is significant that Jehovah God would become a man, never ceasing to be God, so that He could become the Savior of mankind.

   The seventy weeks prophecy of Daniel 9 is of profound importance. Though it is somewhat complicated, it is well worth the time it will take to explain. Key things to remember when explaining this prophecy are as follows: The seventy weeks is a period of 490 years. This time period is divided into at least two parts. The first part is 483 and ends when the Messiah is "cut off." This is the time when Christ was put to death. The 483 begins at the time of the "going forth to build Jerusalem." Bible scholar John Walvoord points out that the time of Nehemiah when the walls of the city were rebuilt was in 444 B.C. It is a very precise 483 years from this date until A. D. 33—the time when many scholars believe the crucifixion of Christ took place. One has to keep in mind that there is a difference in the 360 day calendar of the Jewish year as opposed to the modern 365 day Gregorian calendar. Also, there would be 116 days extra in leap years using the modern calendar (444 B. C. to A. D. 33 = 476 years). 36

Match the following references with the appropriate place on the target: Genesis 3:15; 12:3; 49:10; 2 Samuel 7:12; Isaiah 7:14; Micah 5:2; Daniel 9:24-26.

Table 5: Prophecy on Target

Jewish Calendar	Gregorian Calendar
483 years * 360 days = 173,880 days	476 years * 365 days + 116 days' (leap years) + 24 days (March 5-30) = 173,880 days

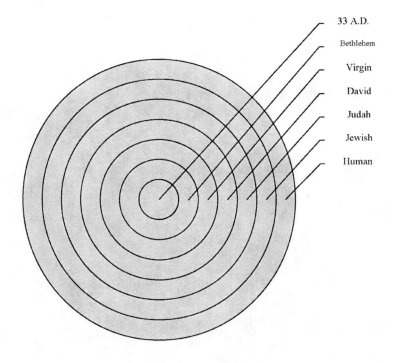

3. Look up the following references and discuss the proofs of Jesus' sinless life: Mark 14:55; Luke 23:22; 2 Corinthians 5:21; Hebrews 4:15; John 8:46; 1 Peter 1:19. Why is it so important that Jesus was sinless?

4. Some have placed the miracles of Jesus into the following five categories: power over nature, power over sin, power over demons, power over disease, and power over death. Do a study through the gospel of Matthew or Mark and record the miracles into separate categories.

Lesson 18
The Most Important Point

Focal Points:

- To defend the resurrection of Christ
- To memorize John 11:25
- To deduce from the established credentials that Jesus is Almighty God

His prediction and accomplishment of His resurrection

On more than one occasion, Jesus said that the temple of His body would be destroyed and that He would raise it up in three days.[37] In spite of the fact that Jesus was being sentenced to death, He prophesied to the high priest that He would one day return in the clouds in great glory.[38]

A few critics have suggested that Jesus may not have actually died at the crucifixion, but this view has no evidence. In fact, all of the evidence indicates that He died—even more quickly than usual by this horrific execution method. This is due to the beatings and whippings He received resulting in blood loss before the crucifixion. The physical trauma of the crucifixion alone would have brought certain death. To ensure a quicker death, the Roman soldiers pierced his abdominal cavity with a sword that went up into His heart. Blood and water poured out. According to one physician, the cause of death was "heart failure due to shock and constriction of the heart by fluid in the pericardium."[39]

There were many witnesses by friends and enemies alike of His death. Roman professional executers pronounced Him dead. He was buried in a borrowed tomb that belonged to Joseph of Arimathea. His tomb was heavily guarded by soldiers.

The evidence for the resurrection is clear. People who look at the evidence will only have a problem accepting it if they begin with an anti-supernatural bias. In other words, those with a truly open mind who look at the evidence will find it very compelling.

The evidence begins with the empty tomb. The proof for this is overwhelming. The Romans wanted Him dead. If the tomb were not truly empty or if the disciples had gone to the wrong tomb, the Romans would have produced the body. The disciples were hiding in fear. They would not have attempted to steal the body. Even if they had, the Roman soldiers would not have allowed that to happen. Their careers, if not their very lives were at stake.

Jesus was seen by more than five hundred witnesses on at least twelve occasions over a period of forty days. He taught, ate, and allowed people to touch Him. People were able to see the scars from the crucifixion. Paul wrote of the resurrection years later and stated that more than half of the five hundred witnesses who saw Him on one occasion were still alive to testify of its truth.[40]

Perhaps the greatest proof of all is the dramatic transformation that took place in the lives of the disciples. They went from fearful and unsure about things, to courageous messengers of what they considered to be the most important truth in the world. Most of them died for their faith. All of them were persecuted. Some people may die for a lie they believe to be true, but no sane person would readily die for something they know to be false. The disciples knew the truth. They lived with Him for three years and then claim that Jesus made multiple post-resurrection appearances to them and taught them many things.

The major arguments against the resurrection and a brief refutation of each are as follows:

1. The disciples went to the wrong tomb. Were they all that stupid? Not only men, but women also went to the tomb to find it empty. Even if they were all that stupid, the Romans and the Jewish religious leaders would have proven them wrong as soon as the rumors of a resurrected Jesus began to spread. This theory does not account for the many post-resurrection appearances or the changes lives of the disciples.

2. *The disciples stole the body.* The disciples were afraid. They were in hiding. Peter had just denied Christ three times. Even if they could have somehow overcome the armed professional Roman soldiers (nearly impossible), they lacked the courage to do so. This theory does not account for the many post-resurrection appearances or the changes lives of the disciples.

3. *The disciples hallucinated.* People see what they want or expect to see. The disciples did not expect to see Him alive. Over five hundred saw Him on one occasion. Multiple people do not see the same hallucination. The writings and teachings of the apostles do not have the feel of testimonies of insane men, but of radically empowered and changed individuals who knew what they saw.

4. *Jesus did not actually die.* This theory proposes that He either feigned death or fainted and the coolness of the tomb revived Him (swoon theory). However, the Roman soldiers were professional executers. They knew how to kill people! Jesus had already died when the soldiers went to break His legs. If He had miraculously survived crucifixion, He would have been far too weak to un-wrap the heavy linens, roll back the stone, and fight off the guards. Besides, He would have appeared as a zombie to the disciples. This theory requires much more faith than simply accepting the testimony of the Scriptures.

Conclusion

Jesus claimed to be God. Since Jesus' claims to deity can be supported by His fulfillment of prophecies, His sinless and miraculous life, and His prediction and accomplishment of His resurrection, there is no legitimate reason to now dispute this claim. Jesus is God. It is up to you to decide what to do with this overwhelming evidence.

Discussion/Assignments

1. Another point could be made concerning the testimony of the disciples of the resurrection. Their message was also confirmed by miraculous confirmation. Go through the book of Acts and try to find seven instances in which the message of the apostles was confirmed by supernatural acts.

   a.

   b.

   c.

   d.

   e.

   f.

2. Jehovah's Witnesses do not believe that Jesus is Jehovah God. Isaiah 9:6 teaches that the Messiah is "Mighty God." Jehovah's Witnesses will agree and state that Jesus is a Mighty God but not Almighty God. Look up the following verses and use them to prove to a Jehovah's Witness that Jesus is Almighty God: Revelation 1:8; 11-18; 22:7, 12, 13, 16.

3. Review the eight points studied so far. See how quickly you can recite. Then try to discuss each point in detail.

4. Watch one of the movies devoted to the life of Christ. List the ways in which the gospel writer demonstrated that Christ was the Son of God.

Lesson 19
The Word of God is True

Focal Points:

- To memorize 1 Timothy 3:16, 17
- To deduce from the twelve points that the Bible is the Word of God

Most of the hard work has been done. The last four points follow logically once the truth of the identity of Jesus is established.

9. Therefore, Jesus is God.

10. Whatever Jesus (who is God) teaches is true.

God cannot lie. Since Jesus is God, He cannot lie. Whatever He says is absolutely true for all people at all times. Any teaching that contradicts His teaching is absolutely false.

11. Jesus taught that the Bible is the Word of God.

Jesus said in Matthew 24:35, "Heaven and earth will pass away, but My words will by no means pass away." He was referring to His own words which are recorded as part of Scripture here in this context. This can apply to all of Scripture if all of Scripture is the Word of God.

Old Testament

Jesus quoted Old Testament passages that are attacked by skeptics today such as the stories of Noah (Matt. 24:37, 38), Jonah (Matt. 12:40), and the writings of the prophets such as Daniel (Matt. 24:15) and Isaiah (Matt. 8:17; Luke 4:17). It is significant that Jesus quoted the prophets because skeptics have tried to place the date of the writings more recent so the books could be classified as historical rather than prophetical, hence supernatural. Jesus acknowledged that Isaiah wrote all of Isaiah and that Daniel wrote Daniel.

One of the most profound quotes of Jesus is found in John 10:35 when He stated that "the Scripture cannot be broken." Jesus is quoting a passage from Psalm 82 in the context of this statement. A close reading of the words of Jesus will reveal that He often quoted the Old Testament more than He gave new teachings. He once said, "Do not think that I came to destroy the Law or the Prophets. I did not come to destroy but to fulfill. For assuredly, I say to you, till heaven and earth pass away, one jot or one tittle will by no means pass from the law till all is fulfilled."

New Testament

The gospels present the history of Christ on earth. The entire New Testament was written years after the events took place. Jesus assured His disciples that the Holy Spirit would bring back every detail to their minds that would eventually be written down and become part of Scripture (John 14:26; 16:13). Although Luke was not one of the original twelve disciples, Paul referred to the gospel of Luke as Scripture (1 Tim.; Luke 10:7). Luke interviewed many eyewitnesses (Luke 1:2, 3). Peter acknowledged Paul's writings as Scripture (2 Tim. 3:15, 16).

Paul gave further confirmation of the authority of the entire Bible. The most encompassing passage is 1 Timothy 3:16 which states, "All Scripture *is* given by inspiration of God, and *is* profitable for doctrine, for reproof, for correction, for instruction in righteousness." The phrase "inspiration of God" means literally "God-breathed."

The Bible is both the words of man and the words of God. The Bible has over forty writers, but only one Author. His Spirit moved men to record the words that would become Scripture. 1 Peter 1:21 says, "for prophecy never came by the will of man, but holy men of God spoke *as they were* moved by the Holy Spirit."

Since Jesus is God, everything He says is true. He clearly taught that the Bible is the Word of God. Since God cannot lie, then everything that the Bible teaches as truth is true. This is not to say that everything is to be understood in its most literal sense. Like many works of literature, the writers of the Bible employed a variety of writing styles to communicate truth. It has been said that all Scripture is literally true, but not all of it is true literally. We must acknowledge the use of figures of speech and cultural nuances of biblical times.

12. Therefore, it is true that the Bible is the Word of God (and anything opposed to it is false).

The Bible is the standard by which all other truth claims are measured. Skeptics will call this view of the Bible narrow-minded. They are correct. However, the hypocrisy in this accusation is that they are also being narrow-minded—by claiming that their own truth claim is right and that other claims regarding truth are wrong. Anyone who claims to know anything is narrow-minded in the sense that what he claims to know, he views as true. Anything in contradiction to this claim he views as false, if he is logically consistent.

It is important to establish one essential truth claim of the Bible at this point. Jesus stated in John 14:6 that He is the way to the Heavenly Father. The apostle Peter confirmed this in Acts 4:12. Jesus' finished work on the cross is the basis of all who obtain salvation. Any other religion that denies Jesus Christ as the way to the Father in Heaven is a false system. Even though that system may have value as well as some truth, the system as a whole falls short of being a standard that can be trusted without qualification.

Go back in your mind to the foundational verse of this study, 1 Peter 3:15. This is a clear command. Christians should prepare themselves to be able to tell others why they believe what they believe. When asked why you believe, you should be able to defend your faith with confidence and clarity. Yet, you should do so in a spirit of humility and respect for the other person.

Do not be intimidated when someone has a question that you cannot answer. Maintain your poise and use that situation as motivation to do further study. This is only an introduction to an exciting lifelong endeavor.

Discussion/Assignments

1. The death of Christ is the basis for all those who go to Heaven. However, Old Testament saints like Abraham and Moses did not know who Jesus Christ was. They had faith in Jehovah God and they were considered God's children. Most Christians believe that when young children die, that they are safe and will go to Heaven. Yet, they have not consciously believed in Jesus as the Son of God and their savior. How do these points relate to Jesus' claim in John 14:6?

2. The fact that Christianity is the only true religion should not bring a sense of pride to believers. The only reason a person can be a Christian is because someone shared the gospel message with them. Brainstorm about ways in which high school students can better reach their generation for Christ.

Focal point: Remember that truth is narrow by its very nature. You should not feel intimidated by accusations of bigotry or narrow-mindedness. You should understand that Satan is doing his best to destroy the church and shake the faith of every believer. He is using the media, educators, and some of your peers to do so. This must be an unwavering conviction.

3. On a separate sheet of paper, in essay format, write about the superiority of the Christian view of loving your neighbor verses the secular idea of tolerance.

TRUTH IN FOCUS

UNIT FIVE

PRE-EVANGELISM AND EVANGELISM

Lesson 20
The BASIC Approach
to Reaching Anyone

Focal Points:

- To memorize the acrostic outline for the BASIC Approach to Reaching Anyone
- To compare and contrast Christianity with other faiths
- To read and meditate on 1 Corinthians 9:22, 23

There have been occasions in which I have actually been ashamed to admit that I was a Christian. My shame had nothing to do with Jesus or the gospel message. My shame stemmed from the public perception of Christianity as a result of the reputations of so many Christians. Some Christians equate being a good Christian with being aligned with a certain political party. Others ride an extreme legalistic horse and judge everyone else over petty issues. Many have a pretty good understanding of Christian beliefs, but have no tact in sharing their faith with others. It is no wonder that so many outside of the church have no desire to enter into a serious discussion about Christ.

The BASIC approach is a simple acrostic to help one remember some of the key ideas that should come up in a conversation with a non-Christian. This outline can be adapted to reach virtually anyone who is opposed to Christianity, yet willing to listen and develop a friendship of trust. It is a pre-evangelism model that can be used to help prepare a person to receive the gospel message, especially those who have distorted or mistaken ideas about Jesus Christ.

In many ways, it is more of a philosophy than a method. No one method is right for every evangelist or potential convert. Yet, it is safe to say that the principles that this acrostic is built on are always appropriate. Each point is built on truth from the Bible, as well as a basic understanding of apologetics. The BASIC approach is as follows:

Benevolence

Show acts of kindness. Demonstrate the love of Christ found in the command to love your neighbor, even when that neighbor is an enemy. Build a friendship of trust with the person whom you are trying to reach. When you do this, you are following the model of Jesus. He developed close relationships with fishermen, tax collectors, and even prostitutes. He so closely associated with sinners that he was accused of being a drunkard and a glutton.

It is time for Christians to begin befriending people instead of judging them. We must love them, not just in theory, but in deed. Loving them in deed may mean baking a loaf of bread for a neighbor or feeding the poor. True love will lead to compassionate actions without expecting anything in return. We should love people even if we think there is no hope of ever getting a chance to tell them about Jesus.

People are becoming more suspicious of the motives of Christians. This is especially true when we do something nice for them only so we can tell them that they are lost or wrong. Only when a person is open or gives you permission should you discuss with him or her the rest of this acrostic. If you never get to go beyond this point with someone, do not despair for you have shared with them the most important point—one of love and compassion. In this way, you have shared the heart of the law and the heart of the gospel.

Almighty God—Absolute truth

You will adapt this point to the person's beliefs you are trying to reach. Orthodox Muslims and Jews already believe in the concept of one almighty and personal God who is sovereign over the universe. They also believe in the concept of absolute truth, but it would be wise to spend a few minutes at least dealing with this point since so many in this culture from all religious backgrounds have rejected the idea of absolute truth. Atheists will differ on the issue of truth. All of them will likely reject the idea of moral absolutes since they reject the only logical foundation for moral absolutes—God.

New Age and Eastern religious adherents will have a different view of truth. Truth is not important to people from an eastern philosophical or religious perspective. The same could be said for many people in postmodern Western culture. Their denial of truth should not intimidate, nor should it anger you. Be patient with them and share your view of truth in a tactful and non-abrasive manner. If no point of agreement can be made, then attempt to share your view of the Bible within the context of their worldview.

Scripture's reliability

Discuss the fact that the original documents as well as the copies of the New Testament are historically accurate. It is safe to say that no writing from the ancient world is as strongly supported for accuracy and authenticity as the New Testament. It correctly records historical events. It was entirely written by eyewitnesses or by those who were well-acquainted with eyewitnesses. It is not necessary to prove that every word of Scripture is accurate at this point. Most importantly, one needs to believe that the Bible is a reliable testimony to the person and work of Jesus Christ.

Hebrews 4:12 states that the Word if God is alive and powerful. There is a dynamic element to the Bible that has the power to open the eyes of unbelief. This is true regardless of a person's worldview. If the Holy Spirit is working on someone's heart, the Sword of the Spirit (the Bible) is effective in producing faith. Just getting someone to read the gospels is a major step in the right direction.

Identity of Christ.

Discuss the person and life of Jesus Christ. To Christians, He is the central figure of human history. Point out the uniqueness of His claims to deity as well as His sinlessness. Once the identity of Christ is established, a person can be pointed to the Bible for the gospel message. If a person is still not convinced, try the last point of "contrast." The following two lists of references can be used to prove the deity of Christ. You may want to list these references in the back of your Bible for easy access.

1. John 1:1; 5:17, 18; 8:58; 10:30; 11:25; 20:28. Read these selections from the gospel of John and explain the surrounding context to the person you are trying to reach.
2. Isaiah 44:6; Revelation 1:8-18; 22:13-16. Together, these verses prove that Jesus Christ is Jehovah, Almighty God, the first and the last, and the Alpha and Omega.

Compare/Contrast

If you have not already done so, find common areas of truth. This is what Paul did in Acts 17 with the Stoic philosophers before he revealed to them the fact of the resurrection of Jesus Christ. Paul actually quoted some of their own philosophers without acknowledging any differences. He indirectly compared Zeus with the Judeo-Christian God.

Be warned that many religious groups use terminology that you will recognize, yet attach to the terms non-biblical meanings. For example, the Mormons will say that they believe that Jesus died for their sins. Yet their understanding of Jesus and the atonement is different than that which the Bible clearly teaches and different from what historic Christianity has always proposed.

In a spirit of humility, contrast the belief system of the person you are witnessing to with Christianity. This is what Paul did when he introduced the idea of the resurrection, a doctrine that the Stoic philosophers vehemently disagreed with. Christianity is a religion of relationship, forgiveness, and joy in this lifetime and eternal bliss in the next. No other religion quite measures up to these claims. A major distinctive of Christianity is that it is rooted in the idea of the work of Christ. We enter into a relationship of God by grace through faith in what Christ did. We do not have to earn our way to Heaven. We then should live a life of good works motivated by our love for God and people. Other religions tend to emphasize works before faith—a system of earning salvation.

Here is a simple challenge to give to people who do not believe in God. If the believer is wrong and the atheist is right about the existence of God, it will not matter when this life is over. Life is short; then we die. The bodies will return to dust and there will be no conscious human life remaining. Yet if the God of the Bible is real, the believer will enjoy Heaven for all eternity and the atheist will be lost. From an eternal perspective, one has nothing to lose and everything to gain by believing in God. The atheist has nothing to gain and everything to lose on his side of the wager. This is sometimes referred to as Pascal's wager, named after the philosopher Blaisé Pascal.

Discussion/Assignments

1. Try adapting the BASIC acrostic to different religious viewpoints and beliefs. Go back to previous lessons and fill in a few main points that you would like to remember long after this class is over and fill them in below:

Benevolence:

Absolute Truth-Almighty God:

Scriptures Reliability:

Identity of Christ:

Contrast:

2. Practice various scenarios. This second suggestion may take up to a week. If you lack this much time in your schedule, try the first suggestion.

    Suggestion 1: A leader should role play certain scenarios and have others try to share their faith with him or her.

    Suggestion 2: choose a scenario either individually or as a group. Research your scenario on the internet or in the library. Learn about the basic beliefs of the person in your scenario. Formulate a plan using the BASIC outline to reach that person. Below are some suggested scenarios. You may decide to make up your own.

#1: You are on a plane on a long flight heading home. The person beside you on the plane is a Muslim who seems interested in talking to you. At first you are nervous to find out that he is a Muslim, but after a few minutes of conversation, you realize that he is not a fanatical terrorist. Later in the conversation, you find out that he is a doctor who lives in your neighborhood. You sense the Holy Spirit leading you to witness to this man, but you do not know where to begin. Then you remember in Bible class. . . .

#2: A new kid begins attending your youth group. He was invited by a member of your church who gives him a ride each week. His parents are not Christians, and he claims to be an atheist. Yet he enjoys coming to youth group because the people there are nice to him. Besides, he does not have many friends and his parents never have time for him.

#3: Your brother has a new girlfriend. They seem to be getting serious. You are concerned that your brother is dating someone who is not a Christian. As you get to know this girl better, you begin to get a burden for her spiritual condition. She is only two years older than you. Perhaps you could reach her if only. . . .

#4: You know a person who says that he is a Christian, but that he does not really believe everything in the Bible. He likes to party and have a "good time." You invite him to church and he seems to have no interest. You ask him a few questions about his beliefs and the more you hear, the more you realize that he is not a true Christian. He believes that Jesus was a wise man of God, but not necessarily the Son of God.

Lesson 21
The Gospel Presentation

Focal Points:

- To summarize the essential points of the gospel
- To share my testimony in written form
- To memorize Romans 1:16, 17
- To examine my faith in the spirit of 2 Corinthians 13:5

Sharing the gospel can be an intimidating task. Jesus told his disciples to preach the gospel and make disciples of people from every nation. Once a person comes to the realization that Jesus is God in the flesh, the last four points of the twelve points from lesson five are easy to accept. It is important to have a good understanding of the essential elements of the gospel. These are found in 1 Corinthians 15:1-5 which states,

> Moreover, brethren, I declare to you the gospel which I preached to you, which also you received and in which you stand, by which also you are saved, if you hold fast that word which I preached to you -- unless you believed in vain. For I delivered to you first of all that which I also received: that Christ died for our sins according to the Scriptures, and that He was buried, and that He rose again the third day according to the Scriptures, and that He was seen.

The gospel is simply defined as the death (for sins), burial, and bodily resurrection of the Lord Jesus Christ. Though the term "gospel" simply means good news, the gospel which Paul had preached to the Corinthians was specifically related to the good news of spiritual salvation. The Corinthians who were reading this letter were already believers. There were some things that Paul did not explain in this definition of the gospel; however, when looking at the overall context of the entire New Testament, the following four questions summarize the essentials of what it takes for a person to become a Christian:

1. Do you believe in the existence of a personal God, and that Jesus Christ is God?
2. Do you acknowledge that you are guilty of sin before God?
3. Do you believe that Jesus died in history, on the cross as a substitute, and that He completely accomplished the punishment against sin?
4. Do you trust Christ completely for the forgiveness of your sins based on his completed work (which includes the resurrection) on the cross?[41]

Most of apologetics focuses on defending the first of these four points. If this point is not understood or believed, the remaining points do not seem as important. God and the identity of Jesus Christ must be believed in the biblical sense of those terms. The concept of sin must also be understood at this point. The crucifixion of Christ does not seem adequate to pay for the sins of the world unless there is a God, that Christ is God, that sin offends God, and that one needs forgiveness by God.

The Importance of Relationship

Too often, people have been rushed into saying a "sinner's prayer" without truly understanding the gospel message. There are people walking around today claiming to be "saved" because they said a prayer, or walked down an aisle in church, or joined a church, yet have no relationship with God. A relationship with God is similar to a relationship with any other person in that it continues beyond an initial meeting. One could not claim to have a relationship with the president of the United States unless she knew him on a personal basis. This is true of the president's spouse or friends or close staff members in the white house. This is not true of someone who happens to shake the president's hand at a campaign rally.

God desires a relationship with his people. He wants us to consult with him before making decisions. He wants us to spend time with him in prayer and meditation. One enters into this relationship when he trusts in Christ as savior. If you are currently trusting in the saving power of the gospel of Christ, then you are in this relationship. You are aware of His abiding presence in your life. There are times when this presence may seem more real to you than others; however, as you grow in the faith, His presence becomes more real to you.

Prayers have often been used to lead person into a relationship with Christ. These prayers may have their place in evangelism, but they can sometimes be a bit over-simplistic. Overzealous believers may be tempted to rush someone through a prayer before a person is ready. We must never forget that it is God that justifies. It is His Holy Spirit that produces faith in the heart of the believers. I cannot do anything or say anything to make this happen. A prayer does not save a person. The "sinner's prayer" is not even necessary for salvation. It is Christ that saves on the basis of His work and grace. However, a prayer can be a helpful expression of one's faith in Christ. If a person truly understands and believes, and chooses to pray this prayer, then salvation has likely already happened. The prayer becomes a memorable experience which a believer learns to associate with his salvation.

For the one who is trusting in Christ, a good verse to memorize and claim for assurance of salvation is John 5:24: "Most assuredly, I say to you, he who hears My word and believes in Him who sent Me has everlasting life, and shall not come into judgment, but has passed from death into life."

Discussion/Assignments

1. Practice writing the story of how you came to know Christ as Savior. Your life story should include information about what

you believed before and after your conversion. Use at least one Scripture reference. Then share your testimony to someone else or in front of a group.

2. Go back and review your testimony. Try to read it from the perspective of someone who has never been exposed to Christianity before. Make changes so that a person with no exposure to the Bible can understand all the terms. Be careful about terms and phrases such as "saved" or "surrendered my life." These will not have the same meaning to other people as they do to you.

Think: The point here is that a person should be sensitive to whom they are speaking to when sharing their testimony. Though the facts of a person's testimony are absolute, the manner in which these facts are shared will depend on the audience's age, culture, and religious experiences.

3. Read 2 Corinthians 13:5. Why would Paul challenge the Corinthians to do this since Paul had been addressing them all along as if they were believers?

TRUTH IN FOCUS

UNIT 6

RELATED ISSUES

Unit 6: Related Issues

Lesson 22
The Problem of Evil

Focal Points:

- To refute false views regarding the existence of God and the reality of evil
- To defend the biblical view regarding the existence of God and the reality of evil

The fact that evil exists in this universe has given many people reason to reject God's existence or attack His character. There are basically four options related to the dilemma of the existence of evil and God:

1. The theistic God must not exist, for if He did, He would not allow evil to exist.
2. God exists, but is not all-powerful. In other words, because of His goodness, God desires to stop evil, but He is unable to do so.
3. God exists, and is able to stop it, but is not all-good, and chooses not to stop it.
4. God exists. He is all-powerful and all-good, but He allows evil to exist to accomplish a higher purpose.

If the fourth option is true, is it possible for humans to know this higher purpose? Is it something about which humans should speculate? Should we just accept what the Bible teaches concerning God's omnipotence and benevolence and disregard the first three options?

First of all, evil must be defined. *Webster's Dictionary* defines evil as something "bad or wrong on purpose; wickedness; sin." It defines "bad" as something "not good; not what it should be."[42] Neither of these definitions is very specific. A better definition is "a privation of good."

1. The theistic God must not exist, for if He did, He would not allow evil to exist.

Theism has already been proven to be true in this text, eliminating the first option as a possibility. The reality of evil actually strengthens the evidence for God's existence. If the theistic God does not exist, then there is no objective absolute standard to determine what is right and what is wrong (the moral law). People instinctively know that some behaviors are better than others because God has written His law in their hearts (Romans 2:14, 15). The existence of evil re-enforces the idea that God does exist. Option one is not possible if there is such a thing as evil.

2. God exists, but is not all-powerful. In other words, because of His goodness, God desires to stop evil, but He is unable to do so.

Option two suggests that God is loving and good, but that He is not all-powerful. He would stop evil if He could, but He cannot. This option views God as finite rather than infinite. However, a God that is powerful enough to create the universe must be powerful enough to have some measure of control over it. To suggest that the Creator of the universe could not stop a dear old lady from suffering from cancer seems ridiculous. The greatest miracle of all is the creation of the universe. To put a stop to certain evil acts, like the September 11th terrorist attacks, would require less power in comparison.

Furthermore, to hold to option two requires one to ignore what the Bible says about God in this area. The Bible teaches that God is omnipotent in a number of passages. Jesus said in Matthew 19:26

and in Luke 1:37 that with God, all things are possible. The term "omnipotent" is used of God in Revelation 19:6. Biblically speaking, option two is not possible.

3. God exists, and is able to stop it, but is not all-good, and chooses not to stop it.

One of the most fundamental ideas about God is that He is good. A God that is not good is not deserving of worship. A God that is not good cannot be trusted. This text has proven the theistic God to be true. The theistic God is eternal, personal, and infinite. He is also a moral being. This is apparent because of the moral law. It seems unreasonable to suggest that God would demand a level of morality in His creatures that He has not mastered Himself.

This view is also in conflict with Scripture. The Bible says that God cannot lie in Titus 1:2 and Hebrews 6:18. The Bible teaches that God is holy throughout the Old and New Testaments (Lev. 11:44; 1 Peter 1:16). James 1:13 says that God cannot even be tempted with evil. Other references include Psalm 22:3, Matthew 5:48, and 2 Corinthians 5:21.

4. God exists. He is all-powerful and all-good, but He allows evil to exist to accomplish a higher purpose.

The fourth option is the only possibility left. Yet, it is still difficult to grasp why God would allow evil to exist. There are several points that should be made here.

1. Sin is a direct result of human and angelic rebellion. God did not create sin. Sin came into this world through the choices of Adam and Eve.
2. Evil came into existence because of the gift of free will. Humans have rebelled against God. God allowed His creatures to choose evil, but did not force them to. It has been said that forced love is rape. God will not force His creatures to love Him. Evil is a byproduct of free will.
3. The reality of evil gives humans a deeper understanding of goodness in the same way that opposite colors accentuate

each other. Sometimes the best way to help someone understand a term is to contrast it with its opposite.

4. Since evil is a privation of good, its reality should drive man to appreciate goodness more, just as the lack of food makes a person appreciate food more.

5. God sometimes uses evil to accomplish a good purpose. Geisler has written, "A drowning person may inspire acts of bravery. . . . God in his providence is able to redeem much (if not all) good out of the evil byproducts in the world."[43] C. S. Lewis wrote that pain is God's "megaphone to rouse a deaf world."[44] Part of God's plan for our lives includes ministry to help alleviate suffering in this world. This sort of ministry would not be possible in a perfect world.

6. Since God is all-knowing, there must be a good reason that He has chosen to permit evil to exist. Just because humans cannot always see a reason for evil does not mean that there is not a good reason. Paul wrote in Romans 11:33, 34: "O the depth of the riches both of the wisdom and knowledge of God! How unsearchable are his judgments and his ways past finding out! For who hath known the mind of the Lord? Or who has been his counselor?"[45] Hebrews 11:3 states that God made the worlds with His word. This is incomprehensible to human understanding, yet it is a basic teaching of Christian theology. Though the Christian faith never contradicts reason, sometimes it goes beyond human ability to understand.

7. The Bible teaches that evil will eventually be defeated. Just because we happen to be living in a time in which evil is a reality should not cause us to assume that things will always be this way. God will eventually separate all evil creatures from all good ones. In this way, evil will be overcome without destroying free will. Compared to the rest of eternity, this period in cosmic history in which evil is rampant is relatively short.

It is possible that God could have created a world in which sin or evil would never occur. However, **an all-knowing God chose to allow evil because He knew that this would be the best of all**

possible worlds—a world in which creatures could choose to love or reject Him. God must consider a world with free will (with evil as a byproduct) as a better world than one without free will. It is difficult to understand this truth. If humans could understand all of God's ways, then God would not be God. The fact is, God is all-good and all-powerful, but allows evil to exist to accomplish a higher purpose. As demonstrated in the above points, even evil can bring glory to God.

The above reasons provide a basis for helping us to understand why evil exists. However, it is ultimately a test of faith. There is a greater opportunity for faith in an evil world than in a perfect world. Do you believe the Bible when it says that God is good? Do you believe the Bible when it says that God is all-powerful? Without faith, it is impossible to please God (Heb. 11:6).

Discussion/Assignments:

1. What is a good definition of evil?

2. How does the reality of evil strengthen the moral argument for God's existence?

3. Look up the following references and consider how each passage can be used to demonstrate that God is omnipotent.

   a. Jeremiah 32:17
   b. Psalm 115:3
   c. John 19:11
   d. Philippians 2:12, 13

4. What does it mean to suggest that God created the best of all possible worlds? This is a world that includes free will and evil as a by-product of free will.

5. Discuss world events that have happened within the past few years that you believe are related to evil or the curse of sin.

Think of ways that God may have brought good out of these events.

Recommended Reading

C.S. Lewis, *The Problem of Pain*

Lesson 23
The Problem of Hell

Focal Points:

- To answer the objections people have against the reality of Hell
- To prove, using biblical and rational arguments, that Hell is a necessary reality that relates to the holiness, justice, and love of God
- To read and meditate on Ezek. 33:11 and 2 Pet. 3:9

The doctrine of Hell seems so horrific that many have discounted it as an evil myth to scare people into the submission of the church. Others have chosen to just ignore the Bible's teachings concerning Hell. Still others have arrived at the conclusion that if Hell is real, then God must be evil. It is important to establish the truthfulness of the doctrine of Hell in a Scriptural and sane manner.

Proofs of Hell
Rational
It seems to be ingrained in human consciousness that the human soul will survive death. Likewise, most people believe that there is a "better place" for some and a place of punishment for others.

Many people seem to get away with great acts of wickedness on earth. If these acts are never punished, it would be a great injustice. When one looks at a Hitler or a Joseph Stalin, and the great acts of evil they committed, there seems to be no earthly punishment fitting for such individuals.

Furthermore, God is not going to force anyone to love or worship Him. If there are humans who choose to reject God, there should be a place for them after this lifetime. Those who do accept God are promised a world without sin. This would not be possible if the wicked were permitted to have free access to any part of the universe.

Biblical

Jesus had much to say about Hell. For example, in Matthew 10:28, Jesus said that he is able to destroy both body and soul in hell. In Matthew 13:41, 42 the Bible says, "The Son of man shall send forth his angels, and they shall gather out of his kingdom all things that offend, and them which do iniquity; And shall cast them into a furnace of fire; there shall be wailing and gnashing of teeth." Other examples in the gospels include Matthew 5:22; Mark 9:47, 48; Luke 12:5; and Luke 16. Revelation 1:18 teaches that Jesus is the one who has the keys of hell and death.

Hell is real. Though we do not know exactly what Hell will be like, we know from the metaphors used in Scripture that it is a place of separation from God. It is a final place. It is a place of suffering. It is a place of outer darkness.

Objections:

1. Why would a loving God create such a horrible place such as Hell?

The Bible teaches that God prepared Hell for the devil and his angels (Matt. 25:41). It is not a place made for humans. Heaven is a place prepared for humans (John 14:2). C.S. Lewis writes about how humans will become more human in heaven and less human in hell. When Jesus said that He was able to destroy both body and soul in Hell, besides making a claim to have authority over life and death, Jesus causes us to ponder what he meant by the word destroy. This is not the same thing as the doctrine of annihilation in which the human ceases to exist entirely. Lewis offers his insight on this subject and writes that nothing can truly be destroyed in the sense of annihilation, only changed. A log burning is destroyed, yet the remains of it go on in the states of gases, ashes, and heat. Human souls may be destroyed in Hell, yet the remains of the soul, of what once was a human being, will remain as something less than fully human, yet something nonetheless.

God does not take any pleasure in the death of the wicked (Ez. 18:23). Hell is the final dwelling place for those who reject His love. It is possible that to some extent humans create their own Hell by their rejection of God's love. There must be a place for those individuals who adamantly and finally reject God. To reject God is to reject all that is godly. If God gives the unrepentant sinner what he wants, he will be given an existence void of all things godly.

2. Is God a failure since so many of His creatures end up in Hell?

God's creatures include angels. Two-thirds of all the angels originally created are elect angels. Only one-third rebelled and will consequently, end up in Hell. No man knows just how many angels were created, but this number is without a doubt, astronomically high.

The idea that the vast majority of humans will end up in Hell is not necessarily a Scriptural idea. Most Bible-believing theologians believe that young children and the mentally handicapped will not go to Hell. Though they have a sin nature, they have not willfully disobeyed God. They are considered safe until they reach an age of accountability. Matthew 7:13 states that the way is broad that leads to destruction and many will go that way. This may have more to do with the fact that there are so many ways to destruction than the idea that there will be more people that end up in Hell. Truth is narrow. The narrow gate leads to life.

Although it may be true that most adults will never trust Christ as Savior, it is not necessarily true that most humans will end up in Hell. God is not willing that any should perish. Those who end up in Hell go there because of their own choice—their own free will.

3. What justice is there in an eternal punishment for a finite number of sins?

The punishment against lost people will be fitting. Every sin committed is ultimately against God. God is infinite. If a person assaults an innocent bystander on the streets, the punishment would be less than the punishment for an assault against the president of the United States. The person offended has much to do with the degree of punishment.

The reason the Son of God came to die in the place of sinners was because of this very idea. No mere human sacrifice would have been sufficient to make atonement for sins. The sacrifice was both human and divine. The value of the sacrifice that Christ made was infinite.

4. How is it that people could be happy in Heaven if they know that people they love are in Hell?

The Bible teaches that in Heaven, "God shall wipe away all tears from their eyes; and there shall be no more death, neither sorrow, nor crying, neither shall there be any more pain: for the former things are passed away" (Rev. 21:4). There are at least two possible applications of this verse that may answer the above question.

First, it is possible that God will erase from memory the "former things." These things would include any earthly memories that would result in pain or sorrow.

Another possibility is that the memories of those individuals will be vague and distant in comparison with the awesome realities of Heaven. Believers in Heaven will be enlightened to a degree no human has ever known on earth. The fruit of the Spirit, which includes peace, will be a constant reality. There is a peace that is able to surpass all understanding (Phil. 4:7).

5. How can God send a person to Hell who has never had a chance to accept Christ?

This is a common, but faulty, question. The Bible teaches that Jesus is the light that lights every person who comes into the world (John 1:9). To some degree, every person, besides the mentally impaired and children who die before they are capable of understanding the gospel, receives a measure of truth. Granted, not all people will hear a clear presentation of the gospel before they die. This seems unfair; however, in God's omniscience there is knowledge of whether a person would ever choose him, even if given a million chances. Every chance that is given and then rejected would only increase the condemnation. The fact that some are not given as many chances may not be fair from a human perspective, but may very well be an act of mercy by God.

All persons have the light of creation available to them according to Romans 1:19, 20 and Psalm 19. Yet, people choose to reject this light. People also have the light of conscience according to Romans 2:14, 15. They instinctively know the difference between right and wrong; however, they choose sin.

God will judge a person based on the truth they rejected, not the truth they did not know. If a person responds positively to the light he did receive, God will give him more light. No person who would have trusted Christ if he had more knowledge will die and go to Hell because he did not have that chance. In the end, we have to trust in God, that the righteous judge of all the earth will do what is right.

Conclusion

There is no contradiction between God's wrath and His love. God hates sin. He is holy beyond human comprehension. God is also loving beyond human comprehension. He extends an offer of forgiveness now to all who will receive Him (John 1:12). Jesus said, "Most assuredly, I say to you, he who hears My word and believes in Him who sent Me has everlasting life, and shall not come into judgment, but has passed from death into life."

God is just. No one will go to Hell that does not deserve it. Furthermore, no one will go to Hell that has not knowingly rejected the truth that God has made available. It is not up to human beings to decide who will be condemned and who will not. God is the just judge. Though the doctrine of Hell can be overwhelming at times, Christians should take comfort in the idea that God will ultimately do what is right. Finally, no one will miss Heaven that has turned to faith in Jesus Christ and His finished work on the cross.

Discussion/Assignments

1. There are some people who have speculated that perhaps there will be a period of evangelism after death for people who did not get a chance to hear a clear presentation of the gospel dur-

ing their lives on earth. Use Scripture and reason to deal with this theory in a group setting.

2. One answer to the problem of Hell is universalism—that ultimately all people will be saved. God will eventually reveal Himself to all people in such a way that they cannot refuse Him. Use Scripture and reason to deal with this theory in a group setting.

3. The objections in this chapter were all in response to the point of view that Hell is real and that some people will ultimately end up there. Besides those listed in this chapter, are there other objections that you have heard about Hell? How would you deal with these objections?

4. Read and summarize Ezekiel 33:11 and 2 Peter 3:9.

Recommended Reading

C. S. Lewis, *The Problem of Pain*, "Hell"
C. S. Lewis, *The Great Divorce*

Lesson 24
The Problem of Evolution

Focal Points:

- To define and explain microevolution and macroevolution
- To distinguish between the ideas of biblical creationism and intelligent design
- To read Gen. 1-3

In the book, *Icons of Evolution*, the writer Jonathan Wells demonstrates how some of the pillars of evolution are false. These "pillars" were supposed to be evidences for the truth of Darwin's theory. Since these have been proven false, why should people now trust the current "proofs" that evolutionists now offer?

An example of one of these former "proofs" is of the Archaeopteryx. This now extinct animal was supposed to be a missing link between the dinosaurs and the birds. It was first discovered in 1862, just after the release of Darwin's *Origin of Species* in 1859. The fossil had wings and feathers like a bird, but also had a lizard-like tail and teeth which resembled that of a reptile.[46] Evolutionists everywhere heralded this animal as a true missing link. However, paleontologists today are no longer convinced.

One of the things that forced scientists to second-guess this theory was the alleged age of the fossil which was not consistent with the date that was supposed to be the time of the transitional forms between the dinosaurs and birds. If the alleged dates are correct, then Archaeopteryx cannot be a true transitional form.

Wells also writes, "There are too many structural differences between Archaeopteryx and modern birds for the latter to be descendants of the former."[47] Modern paleontologists agree with Wells on this point.[48] According to Duane Gish, "no better candidate as an intermediate between reptiles and birds than Archaeopteryx has appeared."[49] Yet it turns out that this animal was simply a bird that has now become extinct. Its feathers are no different than those of modern birds. It possessed a furcula (wishbone) unique only to birds.[50] Evolutionists so badly want Archaeopteryx to be a missing link that they imagine reptile-like characteristics where there are none. Their worldview influences their perception of the data that exists on these creatures.

Archaeopteryx is only one example of many other alleged transitional forms that have turned out to be something different than what evolutionists had hoped for. Even if an animal can be found that seems to bridge a gap between two classes of animals it is important to remember that these classes of animals have been developed by humans. God can create an animal to look any way that He wants it to look. The similarities between animals are more likely related to a common Creator who designed them for a common environment, than a proof for evolution.

It is important to understand the difference between *Microevolution* (adaptations of a particular species to its environment) and *Macroevolution* (a species evolving into another species). Microevolution is true science. The variety of dogs and cats can be cited as examples of Microevolution, even though these animals have been bred by humans and their populations isolated artificially to protect the different varieties.

A natural example of microevolution is the white fur of many of the arctic animals such as the snow hare and the artic fox. The white fur helps the animal to blend in with the snowy environment. In order for changes in a population to occur, changes must take place on the genetic level. In some cases, a recessive trait can become the predominant (most common) trait in a population if that trait helps that species to survive. What helps an animal to survive (such as white fur) in one area may be a liability in another area.

Macroevolution has never been observed. There is no scientific proof for it. Many Biology textbooks appeal to microevolution to try to support the idea of macroevolution. Yet, there is no evidence that the kinds of changes that occur within a species or family could ever result in the kind of major leaps that naturalistic evolution calls for.

In order for macroevolution to occur, very significant changes must occur over a period of time. These changes could never be accounted for by the difference in dominant and recessive genes. It would require a series of genetic mistakes, otherwise known as mutations. Yet, mutations are nearly always harmful. The burden of proof is on the evolutionist to prove that mutations can be beneficial. The magic formula for macroevolution is time + many beneficial mutations = macroevolution. This is not science; at best it is a theory without evidence.

To simplify the theory of evolution into a syllogism, it would look something like this:

1. Given enough time, it is possible that genetic mutations could eventually allow for macroevolution to occur.
2. The possibility of intelligent design is beyond the realm of science.
3. Without intelligent design as a possibility, there are no alternative theories to challenge macroevolution.
4. Therefore, science must come to the conclusion that macroevolution has occurred.

The first premise has never been observed or otherwise proven. The second premise is faulty for allowing an anti-supernatural bias to distort the perception of the data. Many scientists have come to the conclusion that macroevolution has occurred. The only real threat to naturalistic evolution today is intelligent design or creationism. Yet, intelligent design or creationism is not allowed to be a part of the debate by many in the scientific community. This is the present state of affairs in the creation-evolution debate. Evolutionists do not want a level playing field. For them, it is too great a risk.

It takes a lot of faith to be an atheist and believe that the universe has always existed or that it created itself.[51] Both views defy logic. It is much easier to believe the biblical account of creation than it is to believe in naturalistic evolution. All the observable data available to scientists fit better with the creation model than with the atheistic evolutionary model.

Discussion/Assignments

1. Define microevolution

2. Define macroevolution

3. This chapter does not address the difference between naturalistic evolution (atheism) and theistic evolution. There is a major difference in that theistic evolution allows for the possibility that God used a method of natural selection in the creation of the world. Discuss this possibility in light of Scripture.

4. Visit a creation science or intelligent design website and right a summary of an article from the site. Try using some of these key words (or words provided by your teacher) in a search engine to help you find a good article: Institute for Creation Research, Answers in Genesis, William A. Dembski, Michael Behe, intelligent design, creationism.

5. With the help of these articles, try to distinguish between the study of biblical creationism and the scientific study of intelligent design. Compare and contrast the two areas of study.

Lesson 25
The Christian Ethic

Focal Points:

- To memorize Lev. 20:7
- To read and meditate on 1 Pet. 1:13-16 and Matt. 22:36-40
- To compare and contrast the Christian ethic with the non-Christian ethic
- To make the logical connection between holiness and love

1 Peter 1:13-16 states, "Therefore gird up the loins of your mind, be sober, and rest your hope fully upon the grace that is to be brought to you at the revelation of Jesus Christ; as obedient children, not conforming yourselves to the former lusts, as in your ignorance; but as He who called you is holy, you also be holy in all your conduct, because it is written, "Be holy, for I am holy."

The basis for Christian ethics is found in the nature of God—the theistic God who is infinite, personal, holy, and loving. It is His nature from which stems all that can be called good. There are two sources of knowledge of God in this world—general and special revelation. *General revelation* is sometimes called natural revelation. It is available to all mankind. It is the knowledge of God that can be gained by observing nature. It includes the knowledge of God's moral expectations for humans. Every human has an innate sense of right and wrong, even though the particulars are often confused or rejected.

The second source of knowledge of God, *special revelation*, is the Bible. It reveals the absolute moral foundation that every Christian should build on. It is reflective of God's nature. The Bible tells us to be holy, even as He is holy. The Bible reveals that there is an objective difference between right and wrong. Sin is always sin. It is always sin to steal, murder, or commit adultery. It is always right to love.

The Bible also answers the question "why?" in regards to morality. Why is it wrong to steal? Why is adultery wrong? Why is it right to love your enemy? The answer is always related to the nature of God. God's nature is unchanging. He cannot change who He is or His nature. Once a person understands that morality is based on the nature of God, rather than changing cultural norms, then one can see how foolish it really is to ask "why?" It is like asking "Why is two plus two, four?" Two plus two equals four because it is a law of mathematics. It is what it is. The same is true with morality and God. God is what He is, which is absolutely holy. Our ethic must relate to His nature, specifically the attributes of holiness and love.

The Ethic of Love

Jesus said in Matthew 22:37-40 that all of the commandments could be summed up in the two commands to love God and love one's neighbor. Jesus said in John 13:35 that the distinguishing mark of a believer is the demonstration of love amongst God's people. How could love encapsulate all that is morally correct? The answer is three-fold.

    a. The Christian idea of love is not a subjective idea that should be divorced from God's revealed Word.

    b. The Christian idea of love is, and is based on the unchanging nature of God.

    c. God's nature is reflected in nature, and more specifically, the Bible.

Christian love is morally pure. It seeks the best for others. The Christian ethic is not merely a list of do's and don'ts, but a natural lifestyle that grows out of a dynamic relationship with God.

The alternative to an ethic based on the absolute nature of God, is a relativistic, arbitrary ethic. An arbitrary ethic is one that is based on a personal or cultural preference. It will change as the times change. It will manifest itself in many ways. What seems acceptable in one culture is taboo in another culture. Hitler operated on this ethic. So did Gandhi. So do most Americans. Some of these are obviously better than others; however, the tendency with a relativistic ethic is to try to agree on the lowest common denominator—the lowest standard that most people can agree on. The public school system and nearly all of pop culture operates on this ethic. It is destroying the fabric of America as it has brought confusion, division, and frustration.

The only real hope for America is revival on a number of levels. Most importantly, there needs to be a spiritual awakening in which people come to know Jesus Christ as their Lord and Savior. Also, Christians need to wake up from their slumber and take a stand for what is right. Culturally, there needs to be a revival of an ethic that is based on the unchanging absolutes of God's nature. Only then, will the true healing that America needs take place.

Discussion/Assignments

1. Review Rom. 1:19, 20 and Rom. 2:14, 15. Discuss and record your thoughts related to the idea of general revelation.

2. Discuss the differences between precept (absolute truth revealed by God) and principle (deduced from a precept) and between principle and preference (application of a principle). It is permissible to disagree on preferences and sometimes on principle. Precepts are unchanging. Make three lists on the board giving examples of each.

3. Discuss the following two charts:

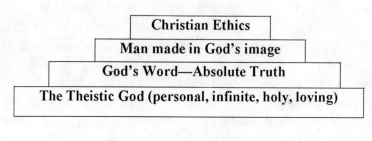

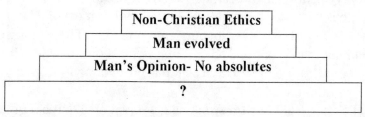

4. List some of the dangerous consequences of choices humans have made because of an ethic that was not based on absolute truth.

   a.
   b.
   c.

5. List some of the possible consequences that could be brought about in America in the future if the culture continues to move away from a Christian ethic.

   a.
   b.
   c.

6. List four important choices that you will be making over the next few years. Then beside each choice, describe how your moral standards should impact these decisions.

a.

b.

c.

d.

7. Read 1 Peter 1:13-16 and Matthew 22:36-40. Spend a few minutes with each passage meditating on its contents. Then write a few thoughts down related to each passage.
Read the Ten Commandments and discuss how naturally people would be able to follow each one if they were able to keep the two Great Commandments.

Recommended Reading

Norman L. Geisler and Ryan P. Snuffer. *Love Your Neighbor.* "Thinking Wisely About Right and Wrong."
Norman L. Geisler, *Christian Ethics.*
Norman Geisler and Josh McDowell, *Love is Always Right.*

FOR TEACHERS

Christian apologetics is a rational defense of the biblical faith. Most Bible colleges and seminaries are inadequate when it comes to training Christian leaders in this important branch of theology. Often students are required to take only one course in apologetics for a degree. The course usually consists of a brief overview of the history of and various approaches to apologetics. Usually the college or seminary takes a stance on one of the systems of apologetics. Often very little practical advice is given for how apologetics can be used by pastors in their churches or by parishioners in their everyday witness.

This is an unfortunate scenario, especially in light of how the worldview of most Americans has shifted dramatically in the last fifty to seventy-five years. Though the intellectual community had begun the shift much earlier, the average American assumed that God did exist and that the Bible was true before the Second World War. The change took place quietly. Churches were not prepared for it. In fact, if churches had been ready for this type of change, perhaps the change would not have been so dramatic.

Today, most Americans do not believe in absolute truth. Though most acknowledge a belief in God, because of their relativistic world view, the concept of God takes on many ideas. The Bible is not viewed as a standard for absolute moral truth. Some of the reasons for these changes will be looked at near the beginning of this book.

Because of this shift, witnessing is a much more complex task. Though it is the Holy Spirit who does the essential work of conversion, God uses humans to spread His truth. Believers are called to witness to specific people in a particular cultural context. The worldviews of the culture being reached will determine how much and what kind of pre-evangelism is necessary. Quoting Scripture to a person who believes that the Bible is the Word of God is very effective. Yet to a person who does not believe in God, or believes that truth is relative, the task is more difficult. The goal is always to get a person to trust in the person and work of Jesus Christ. The path to that goal will depend on where the person is when evangelism begins.

Format

This text is designed as a one semester course. However, for teachers who already teach apologetics and have their own notes, books, and audio-visual media on hand, it could easily be adapted to a two semester course. It is also versatile enough that it could be adapted to small group studies for the home or church youth or college groups.

The text consists of twenty-five lessons with a few practical ideas for assignments or discussion at the end of each lesson. Every Christian school is different, especially in the area of Bible. It has been this writer's experience that students need a good mix of content and practical application. There is enough material for three days of lecture each week. Even lecture days should have some time for practical application. Other days should be devoted to quizzes, tests, practical application, projects, chapel services, relevant videos and whatever else your school decides is important enough to take away from your class time. Lessons are designed so that teachers may move as quickly or as slowly as needed. The material should be reinforced with videos, group activities, and small projects such as those suggested at the end of the lessons. This text is a tool for you to use, not to be a slave to. Sense where your students are and move more quickly, or slowly, as needed.

Lesson objectives are provided in the text. They are listed as "focal points" at the beginning of each lesson. Good objectives are measurable goals for your students to accomplish. You will know your students have met these objectives if they succeed on test day. Feel free to come up with your own objectives as you see fit.

The bulk of this text will be built on a twelve-step practical method of apologetics. Though the exact points have been developed recently by Norman Geisler, the points are based on the Classical approach to apologetics which has been around at least since the time of Thomas Aquinas. Some would suggest that the first record of a theologian to use this method was the apostle Paul when he was preaching to the Greeks on Mars Hill in Acts 17. The logical arguments are often presented in an Aristotelian spirit of deductive reasoning.

One of the goals of all sincere Bible teachers should be the spiritual maturity of their students in their thought life. Though this goal is not easily measured, to help direct teachers in this goal, some of the objectives at the beginning of each lesson will be for students to read or meditate on relevant passages of Scripture. Only the Holy Spirit can produce faith in God and the person of Christ. Teachers can choose whether or not to quiz over the reading of the Bible passages.

The primary purpose of this text is to teach students a practical method of apologetics. The content is well-reasoned and accurate, yet at times, abbreviated. Students should be told that their primary academic goal of this course is to learn the logical progression of this apologetics method, rather than every detail under each point. The method is something they should be able to take with them wherever God leads them in life. It may be used in witnessing situations. It may save some from doubting their faith as they sit at the feet of an unbelieving professor in college.

Course Objectives

1. The students will be able to quote the twelve points of apologetics as outlined in this course.

2. The students will be able to develop an argument to prove each of the major points of this course including the concept

of absolute truth, the existence of God, the reliability of the Bible, and the deity of Christ.

3. The students will be able to apply the twelve points with people of various worldviews.

4. The students will be able to incorporate their knowledge of apologetics in their practice of evangelistic outreach.

5. The student will read, memorize, and apply Scriptures that relates to various points in the text.

Recommendation for Teachers

The study of Apologetics is a lifelong endeavor. This manual is not meant to replace individual study and training on the part of the teacher. Throughout the manual, footnotes are provided so that teachers can readily access more in-depth information from other sources. The more familiar you are with this material, the better you will be able to communicate it to your students, and the better they will be prepared to communicate this material to others. Below is a list of books and other resources to help teachers better prepare themselves to teach such a course.

Copan, Paul. *True for You, But Not for Me*. Minneapolis, Minnesota: Bethany House Publishers, 1998.

Geisler, Norman. *Baker Encyclopedia of Christian Apologetics. Grand Rapids, Michigan:* Baker Books, 1999.

Geisler, Norman L. and Thomas Howe. *When Critics Ask*. Grand Rapids, Michigan: Baker Books, 1992.

Geisler, Norman L. and Frank Turek. *I Don't Have Enough Faith to Be an Atheist*. Wheaton, Illinois: Crossway Books, 2004.

Geisler, Norman L. and Ryan P. Snuffer. *Love Your Neighbor.* "Thinking Wisely about Right and Wrong." Wheaton Illinois: Crossway Books, 2007.

Lewis, C. S. *Mere Christianity.* San Francisco: Harper Collins Publishers, 1952, 2001 edition.

McDowell, Josh. *Beyond Belief to Convictions.* Wheaton, Illinois: Tyndale House Publishers, 2002.

Quizzes/Tests

It is good to test students over your lesson objectives. For example, the main objective for lesson two is to memorize the "Twelve Points that Prove Christianity is True." The quiz or test should ensure that students have committed these to memory. The following are suggested quiz/test questions:

- Scripture memory

- Unit 1: Define terms such as absolute truth, law of non-contradiction, theism, pantheism, atheism, etc.

- List the 12 points. This would be good to do after each lesson. This will prevent students from cramming to remember them right before the quiz. One idea is to have students list them through to the lesson they are on.

- Defend the idea of absolute truth

- Unit 2: List and explain the three philosophical arguments for the existence of God.

- Unit 3: Prove the reliability of Scripture.

- Unit 4: Prove that Christ claimed to be God and defend His claim.

- Unit 5: Share the gospel to an atheist. Share the gospel to a Hindu. Share the gospel to a Muslim.

- Apply the 12 points to various witnessing scenarios.

- Do an in-depth research paper on one of the subjects covered in the course. The recommended readings at the end of many of the lessons can be a guide for students in their research.

Other Grades

- Have students keep a journal throughout the semester. Most lessons will provide a suggested reading from the Bible that relates to the lesson. Have students meditate on the passage and record their thoughts in a journal. Monitor their participation.

- Use discussion/assignment sections for ideas for grades.

Lessons are divided into sections based on units of thought rather than the amount of content. For this reason, the teacher should not feel compelled to fit the lesson into a particular amount of time. Take as much time as is needed until the students have mastered the concepts within each lesson. The section on the twelve points of Christianity could be covered over a period of nine weeks. Some entire days will be spent on application of the ideas with small projects. Some ideas for small projects are included at the end of each lesson.

Teachers should supplement the material with newspaper articles, videos, and other resources. There is a recommended reading list near the end of many of the lessons for those students who are highly motivated. This will not only make the subject more interesting, but will also help the students make these ideas applicable to their lives as they see how these concepts relate to the world in which they live. It is important that teachers help students to move from the theoretical to the practical. Many high school age students will not do this without guidance.

This text is only a brief introduction to each of the points made. Apologetics is a life-long study. Few will master the subject. Yet all believers will benefit from a study of it. It is my prayer that every student in your classroom will have a stronger faith and stronger witness by the end of this course.

Glossary

Absolute truth-something that is true for all people at all times and in all situations; the view that regards truth as fixed or unchanging (See "Truth")

Abstract—something that is not conceptual or concrete; something difficult to understand

Antithesis-the exact opposite of something; contradictory

Apologetics—a rational defense of the Christian faith; a reasoned defense of a Christian's worldview or religious convictions

Archaeology—science devoted to studying ancient artifacts and writings to learn about ancient peoples and cultures

Atheism—a worldview that denies the existence of God

Autograph—an original document; not a copy

Cosmological argument—a philosophical argument for the existence of God based on the existence of the universe and the law of cause and effect

Deity—a god; God; something that is worshipped as divine

Ethics—the study of standards of right and wrong behavior

Finite—Having boundaries or limitations; a being that is limited in existence

Infinite—without boundaries or limitations

Inspiration—"God-breathed;" related to theology, the act of God working through prophets and apostles as they wrote Scripture to ensure that they recorded absolute truth

Irreducible complexity—a single system composed of several well-matched, interacting parts that contribute to the basic function, wherein the removal of any one of the parts causes the system to effectively cease functioning

Law of non-contradiction—in logic, a law that states that opposite ideas cannot both be true at the same time or in the same sense; "The opposite of what is true is false."

Manuscript—a hand-copied document; in the ancient world usually done on animal skins, papyrus, or parchment

Macroevolution--a species evolving into another species

Microevolution--adaptations of a particular species to its environment

Moral relativism—is the belief that regards truth as having no objective basis and that what can be considered right or wrong can vary from time to time, culture to culture, and person to person.

Moral absolutism—the view that regards truth as unchangeable and that what is intrinsically right or wrong can be applied to every culture and time and person.

Multi-culturalism—a movement that seeks to embrace people of various ethnic and/or cultural backgrounds; multi-cultural made up of different cultures or ethnic groups

Pantheism—a worldview that affirms all is God and God is all; God is the universe; God is an impersonal force.

Philosophy—the study of human thought about the meaning of life or ethics

Pluralism—the natural byproduct of a relativistic view on truth that claims all religions are equally valid; all religions lead to God.

Rational—able to reason or think clearly; something reasonable or sensible

Teleological argument—a philosophical argument for the existence of God based on the apparent design of the universe

Theism—worldview that acknowledges a personal, infinite God that created the universe

Tolerance—willingness to allow other beliefs and behaviors; an acceptance of the validity of opposing views

Truth—that which corresponds to the facts; telling it like it is

Volitional—related to the ability to use one's will in making decisions

Worldview—the way in which a person perceives the world in which he or she lives, especially related to philosophical or religious perspective

Notes

1 Kenneth Boa and Robert M. Bowman, Jr., *Faith Has Its Reasons* (Colorado Springs, Colorado: NavPress, 2001), 71.

2 Francis Schaeffer, *The Complete Works of Francis Schaeffer* (Wheaton, Illinois: Crossway Books, 1982), 1:10.

3 Ibid., 10.

4 Josh McDowell, *Beyond Belief to Convictions* (Wheaton, Illinois: Tyndale House Publishers, 2002), 7.

5 Ibid., 7-9.

6 Ibid., 9.

7 Barna Research Group, "Teenagers," Barna Research Online (2001); <www.barna.org/cgi-bin/PageCategory.asp?CategoryID=37>.

8 Barna Research Group, "Americans Are Most Likely to Base Truth on Feeling," Barna Research Online (February 12, 2002); <www.barna.org/cgibin/PagePress Release.asp?PressReleaseID=106&Reference=C.

9 Ibid.

10 Ibid.

11 Ibid.

12 Barna Research Group, "Teens Change Their Tune Regarding Self and the Church," Barna Research Online (April 23, 2002); <www.barna.org/cgibin/PressReleaseID=111&Reference=F>.

13 Norman L. Geisler, *Baker Encyclopedia of Christian Apologetics* (Grand Rapids, Michigan: Baker Books, 1999), 250.

14 Ps. 19:1-5.

15 Rom. 2:14, 15.

16 Stephen Hawking, *A Brief History of Time* (New York: Bantam Books, 1988), 165.

17 Norman Geisler, "Infinite Series," *Baker Encyclopedia of Christian Apologetics* (Grand Rapids, Michigan, 1999), 366.

18 Bertrand Russell, *Why I am Not a Christian,* "and other essays in religion and related subjects" (New York: Simon and Schuster, 1957), 6-7.

19 Neil A. Campbell, *Biology*, 2d ed. (Redwood City, Calif.: Benjamin/Cummings Publishing Company, 1990), 9.

20 Ibid., 12.

21 Michael Behe, *Darwin's Black Box* (New York: The Free Press, 1996), 39.

22 Ibid., 39.

23 Fred Heeren, *Show Me God* (Searchlight Publications, 1995), 196.

24 Stephen Hawking, *A Brief History of Time* (New York: Bantam Books, 1988), 174.

25 C. S. Lewis, *Mere Christianity* (San Francisco: Harper Collins Publishers, 1952, 2001 edition), 8.

26 Dean Hamer, "Are We Born with a God Gene?" *The Charlotte Observor*, October 4, 2004, 17A.

27 Norman Geisler, *Apologetics in a Postmodern World* (Introduction to Apologetics class syllabus, 1997), 48.

28 Ibid.

29 Norman Geisler and Thomas Howe, *When Critics Ask* (Grand Rapids, Michigan: Baker Books, 1992).

30 Geisler, *Apologetics in a Postmodern World*, 48b.

31 Norman Geisler and Frank Turek, *Powerful PowerPoint*, "The Top Twenty-Three Presentations — 12 Points that Show Christianity is True" (2002).

32 Jeffery Sheler, "Is the Bible True," *US News & World Report*, October 25, 1999), 52.

33 Do not be confused by Jesus' statement "You are gods." He was quoting David from Psalm 82 in which David referred to a group of judges who had the authority to make life and death decisions and were thus given a title as a "god." This title in no way implied deity in Psalm 82. This is clear when David states that they would die like men at the end of the chapter. Jesus' claims for Himself went beyond a mere title. He was referring to His identity. For further study on this point see Norman L. Geisler and Thomas Howe, *When Critics Ask* (Grand Rapids, Mich.: Baker Books 1992), 417.

34 John 20:28, 29.

35 C. S. Lewis, *Mere Christianity* (San Francisco: Harper Collins Publishers, 1952, 2001 edition), 52.

36 John Walvoord, *Prophecy Knowledge Handbook* (Wheaton, Illinois: Victor Books, 1990), 251.

37 See Matt. 26:61; Mark 14:58; John 2:19-22.

38 Matt. 26:63, 64; Mark 14:61, 62

39 Michael Bere, *Bible Doctrines* (Pensacola, Florida: A Beka Book, 1992), 201.

40 1 Cor. 15:1-8.

41 These points are summarized from Francis Schaeffer, *The Complete Works of Francis Schaeffer, The God Who is There* (Wheaton, Illinois: Crossway Books, 1982), 1:147.

42 Jonathan L. Goldman, ed. *Webster's New World Student's Dictionary* (United States of America: Macmillan, 1992).

43 Norman Geisler, *BECA*, 222.

44 C. S. Lewis, *The Problem of Pain* (SanFransisco: Harper Collins, 1996, orig. 1940 by New York: MacMillan, 1944), 91.

45 *King James Version.*

46 Jonathan Wells, *Icons of Evolution* (Washington D. C.: Regnery Publishing, Inc., 2000), 112.

47 Ibid., 116.

48 Ibid.

49 Duane Gish, *Evolution: Challenge of the Fossil Record* (El Cajon, California: Creation-Life Publishers, 1985), 110.

50 Ibid., 112.

51 A recent book by this same title goes into more depth about this issue, as well as other issues related to this text, for those who would like to read more. Norman L. Geisler and Frank Turek, *I Don't Have Enough Faith to Be an Atheist* (Wheaton, Illinois: Crossway Books, 2004).

Works Consulted

Books

Behe, Michael. *Darwin's Black Box*. New York: The Free Press, 1996.

Bere, Michael. *Bible Doctrines*. Pensacola, Florida: A Beka Book, 1992.

Blumenfeld, Samuel L. *Is Public Education Necessary?* Boise, Idaho: The Paradigm Company, 1985.

Boa, Kenneth and Robert M. Bowman, Jr. *Faith Has Its Reasons*. Colorado Springs, Colorado: NavPress, 2001.

Booth, Wayne C., Gregory Colomb, and Joseph M. Williams. *The Craft of Research*. Chicago: The University of Chicago Press, 1995.

Burrell, Dan and Philip C. Johnson. *Perspectives in Education*. "Comunication—More Than Words." Mukilteo,
Washington:
    WinePress Publishing, 2000.

Burrell, Dan, Philip C. Johnson, and Paul Tatham. *Perspectives in Education*. "Focus On Parent and Student Relationships." Mukilteo, Washington: WinePress Publishing, 1997.

Campbell, Neil A. *Biology*. 2d ed. Redwood City, Calif.: Benjamin/ Cummings Publishing Company, 1990.

Clark, Robert E., Lin Johnson, Allyn K. Sloat, eds. *Christian Education*. "Foundations for the Future." Chicago: Moody Press, 1991.

Copan, Paul. *True for You, But Not for Me*. Minneapolis, Minnesota: Bethany House Publishers, 1998.

Geisler, Norman L. *Apologetics in a Postmodern World*. Introduction to Apologetics class syllabus, 1997.

_____. *Baker Encyclopedia of Christian Apologetics*. Grand Rapids, Michigan: Baker Books, 1999.

_____. *Introduction to Apologetics*. Grand Rapids, Michigan: Baker Book House, 1976.

Geisler, Norman L. and Frank Turek. *I Don't Have Enough Faith to Be an Atheist*. Wheaton, Illinois: Crossway Books, 2004.

Geisler, Norman L. and Joseph Holden. *Living Loud*. Nashville, Tenn.: Broadman & Holman Publishers, 2002.

Geisler, Norman L. and Thomas Howe. *When Critics Ask*. Grand Rapids, Michigan: Baker Books, 1992.

Gish, Duane. *Evolution: Challenge of the Fossil Record*. El Cajon, California: Creation-Life Publishers, 1985.

Heeren, Fred. *Show Me God*. Searchlight Publications, 1995.

Hawking, Stephen. *A Brief History of Time*. New York: Bantam Books, 1988.

Kennedy, D. James. *Why I Believe*. Revised and Expanded. Nashville: Word Publishing, 1999.

Lewis, C. S. *Mere Christianity*. San Francisco: Harper Collins Publishers, 1952, 2001 edition.

_____. *The Problem of Pain*. SanFransisco: Harper Collins, 1996, orig. 1940 by New York: MacMillan, 1944. Little, Paul. *Know Why You Believe*. Downers Grove, Illinois: InterVarsity Press, 2000, orig. Scripture Press Publications, inc., 1967.

McDowell, Josh. *Beyond Belief to Convictions*. Wheaton, Illinois: Tyndale House Publishers, 2002.

_____. *Evidence that Demands a Verdict*. Nashville: Thomas Nelson Publishers, 1979.

Rhodes, Ron. *Challenge of Cults and New Religions*. Grand Rapids, Michigan: Zondervan, 2001.

Russell, Bertrand. *Why I am Not a Christian*. New York: Simon and Schuster, 1957.

Schaeffer, Francis. *The Complete Works of Francis Schaeffer.*

Wheaton, Illinois: Crossway Books, 1982.

Tanner, Daniel and Laurel Tanner. *History of the School Curriculum*. New York: MacMillan Publishing Company, 1990.

Walvoord, John. *The Prophecy Knowledge Handbook*. Wheaton, Illinois: Victor Books, 1990.

Wells, Jonathan. *Icons of Evolution*. Washington D. C.: Regnery Publishing, Inc., 2000.

Internet Articles

Barna Research Group. "Americans Are Most Likely to Base Truth on Feeling." *Barna Research Online* (February 12, 2002); <http://www.barna.org/chibin/PagePressRelease.asp?PressRelease ID=106&Reference=C>.

Barna Research Group. "Only Half of Protestant Pastors Have a Biblical Worldview." *Barna Research Online* (January 12, 2004); <http://www.barna.org/FlexPage.aspx?Page=Barna Update&BarnaUpdateID=156><hUpdateID=156>.

Barna Research Group. "Teens Change Their Tune Regarding Self and the Church." *Barna Research Online* (April 23, 2002); <http://www.barna.org/cgibin/PressReleaseID=111&Reference=F>

Journal Articles

Sheler, Jeffery. "Is the Bible True?" *US News & World Report*, October 25, 1999.

White, Beverly. "A Personal Scope and Sequence." *Journal for Christian Educators*. Fall 2002.

Primary Sources

Aquinas, Thomas. *On Truth*. Translated by J. V. McGlynn. Chicago: Henry Regnery, 1952-54.

_____. *Summa Theologica*. Translated by the Fathers of the English Dominican Province. New York: Benziger Bros., 1947-48.

Aristotle, *The Basic Works of Aristotle*. New York: Random House, Inc., 1941.

LaVergne, TN USA
31 January 2010
171619LV00006B/105/P